Pieces of My Life:

Poems and Song Lyrics for Everyone with Selected Non-Poetry Writings

By ROBT. G. HOSKINS

Copyright © 2025 by **Robert Hoskins**

Studio of Books LLC
5900 Balcones Drive Suite 100
Austin, Texas 78731
www.studioofbooks.org
Hotline: (254) 800-1183

Ordering Information:
Special discounts are available on quantity purchases by corporations, associations, and others. For details, contact the publisher at the address above.

Printed in the United States of America.

ISBN-13: Softcover   978-1-970283-32-7
          eBook   978-1-970283-33-4

TABLE OF CONTENTS

TABLE OF CONTENTS II

TRIBUTE
TO
LANGSTON HUGHES
AN AMERICAN POET

MOTHER TO SON

Well, son, I'll tell you:
Life for me ain't been no crystal stair.
It's had tacks in it,
And splinters,
And boards torn up,
And places with no carpet on the floor--
Bare.
But all the time
I'se been a-climbing on,
A reachin' landin's,
And turnin' corners,
And sometimes goin' in the dark
Where there ain't been no light.
So boy, don't you turn back.
Don't you set down on the steps
'Cause you find it kinder hard.
Don't you fall now---
For I'se still goin', honey,
I'se still climbing,
And life for me ain't been no crystal stair.

TO THOSE WHO SURVIVE

To those who survive
the conflict
of war, unchanged,

with no more comprehension
of right and goodness
than before,

to you I say:
you are the tragedy
of war.

MY YOUTH

Another Saturday morning,
I climbed up in the truck;
working most the day
was just my luck.

We were hauling milk,
hard work on the road,
I didn't like it then,
but I did what I was told.

But that was then,
and this is now.
For I was twelve,
and what did I know.

But I lived my life,
and I changed somehow;
and from where I stand
I love it now.

CARRIED FROM THE RING

I

  F

    E

      L

        L

Like a fallen champion
carried from the ring,
I didn't see the punch
but felt the sting,
and with it flew a dream
on battered wing.

Love had hit me hard
in both the heart and head.
It opened up old cuts
where I had bled.
"You're down, stay down!"
the referee had said.

But I was proud

I wanted to hear the last bell when it rung.
I wanted to hear the words that I had won.
I wanted victory's taste

upon my tongue
I wanted Love to cling
as I had clung

But wisdom to the fool,
it comes so slow,
For I thought Love
1 gentle. easy foe
that only strikes a light
or glancing blow,
that weaves and feints,
and dazzles every sight,
but lacks the stomach
for a real fight.

Instead Love plays
a hard and dang'rous game.
It bides its time
inflicting casual pain.
It hammers at the ribs
and pounds the head,
opening old cuts
where once you bled.
And when your steps and moves
begin to slow,
Love steps inside to land
its cruelest blow.

No, Love is not a gentle,
easy foe.
I learned with pain
the style's just for show.
I became
a casualty among
the many brawlers

Love has overcome,
who did not see the punch but felt the sting
and later learned
their dream has taken wing.

CONVERSATION IN A SINGLES BAR

Sitting in the Red Town Bar
to find myself a girl,
I smiled at the sexy blonde
with
an overhanging curl,
deciding, then and there,
to give my luck a whirl.

The music was a fast tune.
I asked her
if she'd dance.
She scorned my invitation,
there probably
went my chance.

The single life,
I'm thinking,
isn't what you dream.
But, I asked,
"What are you drinking?"
she poured, "Kahlu and cream"

The music
soon stopped playing,
we talked a little while.
I asked if she would leave with me.
She crooned,
"That's not my style."

Then she asked if I were married.
After thinking,
I said, "Yes."
"Are you happy with that status?"
"Oh, my goodness,
take a guess.

"Would I try
to meet new ladies
if my life weren't such a mess?"
"Oh, you cheat."
She sounded angry,
"On occasion I confess."

Then she threw a curve ball at me.
"What's your wife's name?
T-e-l-l the truth!"
Without a hesitation,
I told her
"Margaret Ruth."

She sighed,
"Your wife, no doubt, is waiting,
keeping dinner warm."
I laughed,
"More likely, she's in bed,
brewing up a storm."

"You fool,
knowing that you're here,
she could be crying."
"No Dear,
only if she knew
the drinks I'm buying."

"You men!
You're all alike,
can't keep from lying."
"Amen!"
We had another drink.
I kept on trying.

NANCY

I've taken a fancy
to you, Nancy,
a fancy to your smile.
And as I sit across the room,
I watch you all the while.
I watch your every movement,
the glance you give the room,
the attitude you show to friends,
the postures you assume.

I've taken a fancy
to you, Nancy,
a fancy to your eyes.
And as I sit composing dreams,
I watch you, mesmerized.
I note the way you tilt your head,
the accent in your speech,
the lilt that rises with your laugh
—you are dreams beyond my reach.

I have this fancy
for you, Nancy,
if only I were bold.
I'd shake this fear that grips my heart
in a vise of cold.
I would searched the skies of romance
for every cloud of chance.

I would summon forth my courage
to make the first advance.

I have a fancy
for you, Nancy,
have you noticed I am near?
Have you seen the ways I hesitate,
the subtle signs of fear?
How I pay you small attentions,
a smile now and then?
The fact that I approach you,
and then retreat again?

I must avoid
this fancy
though will my heart obey?
I know from my experience
that I should stay away.
Still, I'm drawn to your circle
like vapors to the sun.
What I pray need be no miracle.
Will you spare a drop of love?

LOVING KATE

Though Ella's Deli
closed at one,
and I think I see
the morning sun,

It's peeking through
the eastern sky,
I just don't want
to say good-bye.

...touch my cheek softly,
tousle my hair,
tell me again, Kate,
how much you care.

That last glass of wine
I should have refused;
it's bad enough
that my heart's confused.

But, one caress,
it sent a chill,
and later on
I'll pay the bill.

...now tell me, Kate,
what I want to hear,
whisper you love me
in my ear.

The movie
that we saw was fun
but regrettably
I have to run.

The morning sun
puts on its blush,
and I have to beat
the traffic rush.

So I'm leaving now
because it's late,
but before I go,
kiss me, Kate!

THERE WAS A TIME

There was a time
her smile
made my heart skip.

There was a time
I listened
for her step.

There was a time
I longed for
just her kiss.

Not now.

DIFFERENT SHADES OF YOU

Different shades of color dance upon the walls.
Different sounds of evening echo through the halls.
Different shades of loneliness,
Different shades of blue,
everything around me
is reminding me of you.

Now the shades of your love fill my memory.
Faded album photographs are all that's left for me.
Other arms now hold me,
yet I forget they're hers.
Other eyes look at me,
but I see only yours.

Different scenes about you surround me like the rain.
Changing shades of color dance within my brain.
The reds, the greens, the browns, the pinks,
and every change of hue,
each in its place, its time, its mood
are different shades of you.

Now the nights when I'm alone,
hopes ebb back anew.
All these dreams invade my sleep
as I reach out for you.

NEXT MAY

Next May,
I hope the dandelions are yellow,
the showers soft and warming,
and Sylvia returns to me
to end my year of mourning.

I'll wait
the coming of the spring birds
and watch the equinox,
anticipate the flowers,
and count the geese in flocks.

I'll stretch
my two arms to her
and reach Heaven's cloud,
and chase away this loneliness
that has me in is shroud.

Next May
I hope is different
than the clouds of May this year,
the chill of wind descending
the haunts her leaving here.

The frost
that killed the blossoms
left the trees all bare,

in sorrow of her going,
they stand in awkward prayer.

Next May
I hope is different
and spring be back in form
when Sylvia returns to me
to end my winter's storm.

She'll melt
the snow of winter's drifts
that block my happiness
and heal the landscape of my hurt
with the gentlest of kiss.

REUNION

The dandelions
are yellow again,
I can't remember
how long it's been.

But summer and Christmas
both are past,
And nothing, including love,
can last.

So, I wonder how
she will look at me
Remembering
how it used to be.

Will she glance
then return her face away,
Or will her eyes
be soft and gay?

Will she take my hand
and hold it tight
to keep me with her
through the night?

Or will I feel
an aching chill
that lets me know
the thrill
she felt is gone...

SYLVIA, GO SOFTLY

Go softly, Sylvia, go
to an enchanted land aglow
with fantasies and dreams.
No place else it seems
can make it so.
Go softly, Sylvia, go.

Dream softly, Sylvia, dream
the night will bring the sun,
then you can let the memories run
like athletes for glory.

Sleep softly, Sylvia, sleep
take back the love I cannot keep,
preserve it as one does a treasure
for a different story.

Sleep softly, Sylvia, sleep
the hill we climb will be too steep,
and I have promises to keep,
So, sleep.

Sleep softly, Sylvia, sleep
my love was true.
Sleep softly,
a thousand miles away I weep
for you.

MY DREAMS

Like the wedding rice
tossed outside of church doors,
my dreams lie scattered on the ground
for sparrows' pickings.

How can I collect
the grains
I so casually discarded
and return them
to the cannister
where I had stored them.

Maybe
some grains the sparrows miss
will lie on fertile ground,
and there sprout roots
when rained upon
and grow.

I know
they would never sprout
in the cannisters
where I kept them.

ONE WAY TO SAY GOODBYE

I asked if she would marry me.
She said, "No!
I'm never going to marry.
So, please go!"

I asked if she would kiss me.
She said, "Wow!
You know I want you out of here,
right now!"

I asked could I at least
have one small hug.
"Get out! You're annoying me
you. lug!

You're arrogant and righteous
which I find hard to take.
Besides, you're argumentative.
Now leave, FOR GOODNESS SAKE!

So I left.
And... I'm never going back.

PRAYER TO ST. JUDE

I've heard of you, Jude,
a powerful dude,
with friends
in real high places.

The word on street
is pretty upbeat,
so I've come to touch
all the bases.

If you are really high up,
you can fill my cup,
it would please the Hell
out of me.

Don't mean disrespect,
but I kind of expect
your friend will say no
to my plea.

See this woman I know
has this wonderful glow,
entrancing,
beyond all my dreams.

She is witty and bright,
a charming delight.

She just doesn't love me
it seems.

So, I come to you now
thinking somehow
you can stop these tears
I've been crying.

But I have to admit,
before you commit
if I said I had hope,
I'd be lying.

SO HAPPY LIVING SINGLE

I can watch TV late at night without some dirty look
and leave the bedroom light on if I'm reading a good book.
If I want to, I can spend the night sleeping on the couch
and not wake up each morning to a cold and snippy grouch.

I'm so happy living single in the middle of my life.
I don't dance to no one's fiddle, who says you need a wife?
So, I'm sitting here, drinking beer, feeling quite content.
I don't have to worry in the world, if she keeps up the rent.

I can leave newspapers on the rug, forget to lock the door.
There's dirty dishes in the sink, my shoes on the kitchen floor.
I can chug milk from the bottle, I don't need to use a glass;
don't need to hear a lecture about my lacking class.

Well, she claimed I hogged the covers, complained to me I snore,
when we were out on weekends, she thought I was a bore.
Now, she's dating some new fellow with his snoot up in the air,
but I don't give a hoot-in-hell, at least I got my hair!

Such a pleasure living single in the middle of my life.
I don't dance to no one's fiddle, who says I need a wife?
So, I'm sitting here, drinking beer, feeling quite content.
Just waiting for that woman to crawl back and repent.

I hope she paid the rent this month.
I'm running out of beer and the dog could use a grooming.

Rover! Get off the couch!
You're spilling my beer.

ARF!

WEARING YOUR RIBBONS AND BLUE JEANS

I drove by your dad's old farm today.
I stopped where we used to park.
Even in the bright sunlight,
the place was empty and dark.

The windows upstairs needed curtains,
the chimney needed some smoke,
The walnut trees in the yard were bare,
the front porch swing was broke.

Still, I remember that August day,
a girl in pigtails came my way,
coming from your father's farm,
a bracelet on her sun-tanned arm,

a girl with a pan of beans,
she was wearing your ribbons and blue jeans.

II

When we were sixteen, we swung on that swing
at night when your folks were asleep.
We kissed and hugged, we whispered so low,
the promises we couldn't keep.

You used to say, "We'll find a way;
we'll have a house and kids."
In innocence, we chased the dream
like teenagers always did.

It's like yesterday in my memory,
a sun-faced girl wearing ribbons and blue jeans.
We had the house, we had the kids,
but something got left out.

In twenty years, the trust was gone,
young love turned into doubt.
The last time that I talked to you,
I saw you with a friend.

We said 'Hello' and reminisced.
You asked, 'How have you been?'
And I thought back to that August day
when a girl in pigtails came my way, —
a girl with a pan of beans,
wearing your ribbons and blue jeans.

LIKE SUMMER IN JUNE

I remember
when I met you
at the airport
late at night.

You were coming back
from California.

...the flowers
and the champagne

...the harbor
filled with lights
of the fishermen offshore

...the chillness
of Lake Michigan's breeze.

It was late April,
but you wore a yellow dress,
like summer in June.

THIS IS THE DAY

This is the day
that I will remember
apart from all of the rest.

This is the day
you made me happy
knowing you loved me best.

This is the day
I was waiting for
and knew you felt the same.

This is the day
you held my hand
at our high school hockey game.

FLY HIGH

When we got back from our trip to LA,
that was the day you sent me away.
You needed your freedom
to move on alone,
free of attachments,
life on your own.

But I gave you caring,
a refuge from strife.
And what did you do?
You flew out of my life!

Then go, free bird,
fly high and fly clear.
I can look at myself in the mirror.
I won't try to hold onto your wings.
I've made up my mind to do better things.

II

O' you let me down easy:
it wasn't my fault.
A very good reference
you gave me, no doubt.

Generous and kind,
Loving, you said,
and that might have felt good
if my heart hadn't bled.

III

Now friends ask,
am I the old me?
How do I feel,
who do I see?

Am I getting along?
Is there anyone new?
Are things going okay?
Do I ever see you?

Not knowing really
how to reply,
I quote them your words
without batting an eye:

"What does it matter,
how do I feel?
Love always ends,
it's not a big deal."

IV

So fly, free bird.
Fly high and fly clear.
I can look at myself in the mirror.

And every time
I look up to the sky,
I say in my heart,

Fly high.

42

WITH MORE PRACTICE

Her eyes were savage,
no longer blue.
"I'm mad because
I'm stuck with you!"

Like a hypodermic needle
stabbing him,
her words left tiny punctures
in his skin.

The pin-prick beads of red
show promise,
more promise than
a kiss.

Now with practice
on her part,
she'll learn someday
to reach his heart.

MARY ANN

MAR-AR-Y A-ANN!
MAR-AR-Y A-ANN!

Her name, it haunts me now.
No matter where I am
I think of her somehow.

I see her
in the traffic lights
—the redness of her lips.

I see her
in a passing train
—the swaying of her hips.

I see her
in the waving trees
—she dances, sways, and dips.

I see her
in the wine I drink
—I draw her love in sips.

II

Leaves that somersault
from trees,

Dolphins leaping
from the seas,

Wind chimes playing
in the breeze

ALL FREEZE!

when Mary Ann
does her t-e-a-s-e
-ing dance.

III

Fat chance have I
to catch her eye
and win her hand in marriage.

I'd have to be
a prince with charm,
six horses, and a carriage.

Still, I think,
I dream, I wish... I can
win the love of Mary Ann.

I know that I
will forfeit bliss
to hold her close, to have one kiss,

to touch her lips,
to taste her tongue,
to follow her if she be won.

IV

I know the course
that I must run.
It leads me closer to the sun,

and then beyond
the Milky Way
to stars that serve to guide my way.

Across that wide
and endless span,
I'll follow them to Mary Ann.

EYES

I was stretching my legs
when my feet touched her
under the table.

"Excuse me!"
I don't often make contact
with people this way.

Ordinarily,
I let my eye
make introductions.
Feet are too clumsy
to make introductions
on their own.

They leave a track of dirt
when they retreat
and sometimes crushed petals.

But eyes,
when eyes meet people,
they can linger long with leisure.

Or turn away.
Eyes never leave hurt toes
or floors that need sweeping.

LOVE'S CALL

Call out the cops!
Call out the judge!
I will confess that I'm in love.

And though a cell awaits my fate,
I'm glad that love at least came late.

Slam the bars!
Hide the key!
A sentence of life is awaiting me.

Sure, Eve led Adam to the Gate.
Did you think I did not hesitate?

So give me bread.
I'll drink the water.
I recognized she was Eve's daughter.

And I know I can't escape my fate:
it's a lesson that I learned too late:

So chain me
with a ball and hammer!
I'll do my time in the Devil's slammer.

Forever grateful for love's call
than never to have loved at all.

48

A Dream Forgotten

She is wine without a cork.
She is tarnish on a fork
—well used china, chipped,
a love-seat sofa, ripped.

Her hair lacks kink
or natural curl,
but I call her my spring-time
dandelion girl.

And though she's not a person
that merits a salute,
my love for her is true
—it's absolute.

What matter if her "Sunday best"
is made of cotton?
To me she is a dream
I had forgotten.

WHY YOU LOVE ME

Did I impress you with my talents?
Did I grab you with my looks?
Did you think that you could read me
like the [ages in your books?

Did I surprise you with my singing
that I never strayed off-key?
Did the fact that I attended church
light up the Grand Marquee?

Did the things I said amuse you?
Were you taken by my flair?
Perhaps you thought mistakenly
I was a millionaire.

Was I behaving like a gentlemen
Was it something that I said?
When I ordered at the French cafe,
did you think I was well-bred?

I suppose it was romantic
when I read you poetry.
The two of us, imagine,
footloose and fancy-free.

The fact that I walked boldly,
straight into your heart,

is that the explanation,
why you loved me from the start?

I haven't got it figured out as yet,
but it happened down in Tennessee, I bet.

I'M NOT IRISH

On a quiet road
late at night,
a chinaman stands
in the pale light
of a street lamp
selling flowers

-- it's St. Patrick's Day

He doffs his paper derby
and he smiles.
Standing in the cold,
he looks too old
to be working
these late hours.

Still, I buy you
two carnations,
green and red.
"Five dolla",
the chinaman said.
Then, "Thank you,
Thank you". (twice!)
"So-o-o nice."
as he put away the money.

But the thing
that I find funny
after I shelled out the money,
is why?

I'm not even Irish!
I am B-R-I-T-I-S-H!
-- and a little Finnish.

UPON BEING BOLD

You're a nice lady.
Do you ever accept dates
from men you don't know?

We could go to dinner
or a movie, or listen to jazz;
or we could sit on a park bench
and watch the squirrels.

I don't want you to think
that I'm being bold or aggressive,
but I never thought timid
got me anywhere.

54

FOLLOW THE TRAIL

I left tracks on her carpet;
that's how I got back here.
They led me to her room.

Hansel and Gretel were smart.
I should drop breadcrumbs
when I leave her.

JOSIE

Josie sits on a park bench,
I watch her every day.
I wonder if she'll talk to me,
I wonder what to say.

Hi! would you like a piece of candy?
Don't the birds sound sweet today?
Do you think it's going to rain?
Would you like for me to stay?

I'm going to talk to Josie
-- open up my heart.
That's the only way I know,
so that's the way I'll start.

DOING SOMETHING RIGHT

We've been together
just about a year.
And every now and then
I catch you you call me 'Dear'.
And sometimes when we're walking,
your hand slips into mine
and smiling to myself, I think:
finally,
I'm doing something right.

IT'S THE ENVIRONMENT

Like wind the mountains turn aside,
our love cannot abide
the walls you build around you.

Like the climate, we're affected
each time that love's deflected
from the heart.

This explain why the rain falls
in other places.

WHEN WE DANCED IN TENNESSEE

When we arrived in Clarksville,
you combed your long black hair.
You put on jeans and perfume,
the scent of country air.
We found our way into Mike's Bar;
He asked, "What will it be?"
A tall one for the lady
and some happiness for me.

Dancing and laughing, you smiled at me,
and when our lips touched, I felt ecstasy.

O' that night, in Tennessee,
stays like a love song in my memory.
The soft lights and your laughter,
the kisses you gave me,
did you fall in love with me in Tennessee?

They served the same Milwaukee beer
in a frosted glass.
The juke box played the same love songs,
one by Mama Cass.
The same old moon hung in the sky,
about the same long distance,
but Tennessee somehow broke down
the last of your resistance.

Now, days and nights have skipped to years,
still we dance with grace and flair,
and every time I'm near you,
I breathe the country air.
Though Milwaukee was a long way home,
about six hundred miles,
I still remember Tennessee,
your soft voice and your smiles.

And how you fell in love with me
the night we danced in Tennessee.

SNATCHES OF THOUGHTS - THREE SHORT POEMS.

DIVERSIFIED INVESTMENTS

I saved caramels for her sweet tooth,
she only ate the cremes.
She invested in the Market.
I invented in our dreams.

IF ONLY...

If only promises would last forever
and flowers did not have to die.
If only friends could come to visit
and never had to say goodbye.

SHE DRINKS

She drinks brandy
from a snifter.

The more she drinks,
the more we differ.

CHANGING HORSES

She told me I should saddle up, comprende?
Take only what I bought, not one thing more.
"Vamos!" is what she yelled when I protested.
Then she kind of helped me find the kitchen door.

Now, I'll shake the dust form my sombrero,
catch my breathe, and roll a cigarette.
I'll think about tomorrow when it gets here,
and tonight I'll find a barstool and forget.

Changing horses, changing women,
it's pretty much the same.
Whenever love goes lame,
I just change horses.

She was always kicking ashes on my fire,
always dumping sand inside my boots,
always looking out for greener pastures,
I knew deep down she didn't give a hoot.

Yeah, I changed horses in my time aplenty.
I'll likely change again before I'm through.
Just give me a horse with lots of spirit.
I kinda like my women that way too.

Changing horses, changing women,
it's pretty much the same.
Whenever love goes lame,

I just change horses.

Somewhere roams a horses that ain't been broken.
I'll rope her with my rawhide lariat.
Then put my brand upon her willing finger
and together ride off to a new sunset.

"Vamos" is what she told me, so I'm going,
and maybe I should feel some remorse.
But things are always changing in this world,
and it's time I saddled up a different horse.

Yeah!
Whenever love goes lame,
I just change horses.

GIFT HORSE

She was a gift horse,
unexpected, but in spite of
the adage against it,
everyone tried looking at her teeth.

Maybe counting her teeth
would determine her value.
Bettors at track side
could not be more critical.

But I saw the way
she shook her head.
I could tell
she'd be a winner.

So I kept her
without looking at her teeth.
What matter is pedigree?

II

From her first wobbly steps,
she wanted her head,
but I thought better the bridle
and grow used to its fit.
Now she is grown,
and she shows at family affairs,

cavorting among the guests
with confidence and grace.

Someday,
I will collect from the bookies.

LOSING HER MARBLES

I watch a marble roll away
as she tells her story again.
I have lost count of the times
that I have heard it.

She lost another marble yesterday.
She paid he telephone bill
a second time,
then missed the doctor visit
she had made.

Still, I remember when her mind was bright,
typing at the kitchen table
lat at night.
She made sure the sentences were right,

No spelling errors for her.
No subject-disagreement with a verb.
Her thoughts were fast,
but nothing lasts.

Now age has its grip.
Each day she takes a smaller sip,
her cup is running dry.
It's Hell to have to watch her die.

TELL HIM HELLO

Take my touch
up to God's altar
and tell Him 'hello' from me.

Tell him I am sorry
I could not come myself,
but please,

not put me
on some shelf
where I will be forgotten.

He might,
my luck has been rotten.

QUO VADIS

Standing by the tomb
one Sunday,
I peered into the gloom.
"Are you in?"
I called to Him.
I came to talk about my sin.
Are you there?

It was Friday
that I heard
the good news going 'round,
I came to check it
out with you,
but now, you can't be found.
Are you there?

Someone told me,
is it true,
doors will open up for you?
All i need
to do is knock
if I want to join your flock.
Is it true?

Some guy with wings
leaned on a sword.
"You must be looking for the Lord.
He has risen

from the dead
and had to hurry on ahead.
So He is gone."

The Occupant is gone,
you say?
He didn't wait for me?
Three days were all
He stayed around
after hanging on that tree?
Where'd He go?

Well, He is gone to save
the world I heard,
to spread His love and cheer.
But a lot of good
that does for me,
He left me standing here.

THE LIFE OF JESUS

Proclamation
celebration
revelation
adoration
consternation
mutilation
exaltation
Our salvation

ODE TO SOMEONE I SHOULD HATE

I hope I read your name
in the newspaper
that they chalked your outline
on some rainy street,
that your blood ran down the gutter
to the sewer,
and the coroner wrapped your body
in a sheet.

I hope that the detectives
miss the motive;
that the witness are blind,
stone deaf, and dumb;
that no one can identify
your person;
that you left this world in stockings
with a run.

I hope your family doesn't mourn
your passing,
that St. Peter turns his back
when you arrive,
that your suffering down in Hell
is everlasting.
just knowing I'm still laughing
and alive.

ALEXANDER'S DISH

The reaper cuts a swath,
the world spins
a turn,

Balanced on an axis,
fixed there
firm.

An innocent mouse
in the field runs
disturbed.

An unknowing boy
stomps violently
unperturbed.

He stoops to grasp
the lifeless form
by tail,

Then nonchalantly
drop it in
a pail.

He's saving it
for Alexander's
dish.

But Alexander
preferably eats
Fish.

EXISTENCE

Existence
is prior to essence
the existentialists say.

I am,
therefore, I think,
there is no other way.

But Descartes
when proving existence said,
"I think, therefore, I am."

If he's correct,
then Sartre is wrong,
or should I give a damn?

If I endorse
the thought of Sartre,
I'm called an existentialist.

If I accept
Rene Descartes,
I'm just another rationalist.

Curse it all
I can't decide
this challenge to my awesome pride.

Yet, does it matter,
must I choose
between the two opposing views?

Perhaps I'll end it all,
then damn,
it will not matter I am.

RING AROUND THE TUB!

Ring around the tub!
"Aye there's the rub,"
I rub!

From where did you
numberless particles
that sought the friendship
of my body come?

Out of infinite time and space,
seeking a home, seeking me?
And I ungrateful
washed myself of thee.

DECEMBER SONG

Lonely bird in the show,
You should have flown south.

The time for building nests is gone.
The time has ended for all song.
What mate will hear a weakened whistle
dimmed by winter's wind?

Too late bird, for planning flights;
for love and summertime delights,
and dreams that beckon.
Upon old age you did not reckon.

OLD GEEZER

I watch as the 'old geezer'
steps cautiously out of his car.
On wobbly legs, he makes his move
to turn around.

Shoulders slightly stooped,
he wears a grayish sweatshirt,
too big for his shrunken body,
and pajama bottoms for pants.

He walks slowly
around the front of his car,
extending his arms
to touch the car for balance.

He had parked his car
near the entrance of the building,
and now he steps up the curb
to the sidewalk.

As he makes his way,
I watch the passenger-side door
open slowly,
and an old woman, with cane,
awkwardly rise from the car seat.

Like a crane or goose
trying to break free
from the waters of the lake,
the woman struggles to raise herself
from the car seat to take flight.

As the woman approaches him,
the old man steps down from the curb.
He offers his arm for support,
and she plants her foot
as if to climb Mt. Annapurna.
After she is steadied,
she grips his arm firmly.
Together, they step forward in unison,
like dancers, who hearing music,
rush to the dance floor
before it ends.

At the building door, the old man stops
as though to check his bearings.
Sadly, they are not heading
to a dance floor -- for them
the music ended years ago.

Today, it is the doctor's office
where they are heading,
and hopefully, he news they hear
will be music to their ears.

WHEN WE WERE YOUNG

When we were young
you loved me best
instead of any
of the rest.

But now, you're different,
not the same,
as different
as 'come' and 'came'.

Like sleet
instead of gentle rain,
'Came' is past,
the present pain.

Now I wait
to hear the ring
of telephone
and your voice sing,

I need you...

PREFERENCES

I preferred marriage
along with a carriage.
She preferred the status quo.

I preferred black jack.
She liked the dice.
Why we gambled, I'll never know.

She preferred classical,
I listened to jazz.
On her scale, jazz registered low.

I ordered the turkey
she wanted goose.
Guess what?

She let me go.

ODE TO SAMARROW CHANEY

In Independent Reading Group,
you usually tried to fly the coop.
You left the room by hook or crook,
but I never saw you read a book.

You must concede
a book to read
can make a person happy.
Just once I'll need
to see you read,
now can you make it snappy?

Because Smarrow,
by tomorrow,
your school days will be ended,
and when I tell you:
read a book;
don't act like your offended.

So always heed
advice to read,
for books can make you wise.
Get with it, girl,
give books a whirl
before you ups and dies.

The Reading Group
which students need
was scheduled so
that you would read.

So this advice
I offer freely:
throughout your life
read books— REALLY!

SOMEDAY I WILL BE HER ROMEO

I watched from the window,
she was running in the snow,
and the sudden thought occurred to me,
could I be her Romeo?
But I was only twelve years old
and too afraid to ask.
Instead, I hid my thoughts from her
behind a teasing mask.

But I said, "Someday I will be her Romeo.
I will warm her hands and brush away the snow.
Someday I will be her Romeo."

II

At eighteen we were seniors,
set to graduate
when I finally found the courage
to ask her for a date.
I said, "I will be you Romeo
if you'll be Juliet."
The smile that she gave to me
I remember yet.

And she said, "Someday you will be my Romeo.
You will warm my hands and brush away the snow.
Someday you will be my Romeo."

III

The day came when we said "I do",
and life took off from there;
until a Saturday in June,
I felt a winter air.
She said, "Dear Love, I have some news.
Come sit here next to me.
I'm not well and now we need
to plan for what will be."

And she said, "Dearest Love, you are my Romeo.
The time has come to warm my hands
and brush away the snow."

IV

On an autumn Monday,
the leaves were red and gold.
I sat beside her in a chair
Until her hands were cold.
Now January's all year 'round,
but I don't see the snow.
I'm still in love remembering
I was her Romeo.

RUSSIAN MUSIC

In the Redlands Bowl,
under a night of stars,
I sit with a thousand other people.

We listen to the Russian master,
Emanuil Sheynkman, master
of the mandolin and balalaika,
play songs of his homeland.

Ruebenstein, Rachmaninoff, Tchaikovsky,
and "Fantasy on Russian Folk Themes
by Sheynkman himself.

Strains of music
emanate from the stage
to fill the night.

Everything is quiet,
except for the music.
Beauty flow from practiced
skill and love,

I am alone.
I am a stranger from another place.
My thoughts are not of here,
but of my own Russia.

Away from family,
and the surroundings of home,
away from Wisconsin,
the music haunts my thoughts.

Russian music is too sad.

SPIRITS

A California woman
is a wisp of memory.
She visits me
when spirits come unbottled.

And like the spirits,
she is gone by morning.

MY ROADS

Just like all roads lead to Rome,
every path I take leads to her door.

UPON HER DYING

The room was dark
except for small lamp
on the bedside table.

My sister lay conscious,
her eyes open,
watching the intimate scene
within the room.

She raised her head slightly
when she saw me.
A smile crossed her face.
Her son, who was at her bedside,
gave up his place without speaking.

She spoke quietly,
and I knelt close to hear.
"I don't know what to do,
whether I should let go."

My eyes formed tears.
"Let go, Nancy, "I said.
"God is waiting for you.
You don't need to stay for us."

She held tight to my hand,
and I began to caress her forehead.
Except for occasional whispers,

the room stayed quiet,
and Nancy fell asleep.

II

Later, when she woke again,
her husband helped her out of bed,
and wheeled her to a place at the kitchen table
where she sat, attended by her daughters.

She looked stronger in a chair.
No talk of death in the kitchen.
We talked about familiar things,
and recounted stories of better times.

Throughout the day, people continued to arrive:
among them our sister Kathy,
her daughter Cherie and family,
and a longtime neighbor.

Together, we reminisced,
laughing and sharing stories.
Nancy listened mostly, and sipped water
as we worked to keep her spirits alive.
But privately, I prayed for God to take her.

Late that night,
after most of us had gone,
Nancy died.

It was 2:37 AM.

She was 64 years of age
in August 2005.

REMEMBER

Do you remember
green carnations
and a foggy road
at night?

And the Chinaman
who stood alone
under the street
light...

the bonnet the
I bought for you
to wear when we
got married,

and the dandelions
I sent to you,
the boxes that
I carried?

Remember
Capistrano,
the bar at
Newport Beach,

the view from
San Jacinto
and the dream
we hoped to reach,

the restaurant
on the mountain
where I sang
and folks applauded

and the happiness
we hoped to share
but somehow
always doubted.

... I remember

THE HOUSE STANDS VACANT NOW

The house stands vacant now,
the chimney breathless,
and at night the wind rises
through the evergreens
vibrating windowpanes,
shaking memories form old stone and wood.

A shutter knocking in the wind
beats the ebbing throb of a heart.
And in the yard where children once had played,
weeds have overgrown the sandpile.
Already the stone of the barnyard wall
is crumbling
while in the barn, a society of sparrows
Occupy the loft.
Occasionally, a homeless dog wanders by,
but somehow a dog knows
the smell of death and does not linger.

In autumn,
people form the city stop to hunt,
asking permission from a neighbor.
The hunters trespass o a family's soul
buried in these fields,
fields that no longer sprout the greenness
they knew. But then the earth is tired
and mourns the hands that stroked it

for generations.
—the hands of a man and his family.

Part II

They took the old man away one day
heedless of his tears,
and now he sits in a home for the aged.
Sometimes he rocks, his eyes closed,
and the attendants think him dead.
But when the sun begins to set,
he rises for supper.

The old man has only memories now:
the times he walked in his land;
the pause in the threshing day
when neighbors passed the cider jug;
the vibrating engine that turned the pulleys
and made the belts of the thresher sing.
And like a pre-historic dinosaur,
the machine vomited straw and the chaff
through its great maw.

There were days with his wife—contentment
—but that was long ago
before she went insane.
She died, not recognizing her brother,
clutching at the bedsheets,
and rolling her eyes in fear.

And there was Cleve, his oldest son,
who stayed to work the land—
a good farmer, respectful of the soil,
giving back to the land
as much as he took from it.

But Cleve's wife left with their children,
and Cleve committed suicide.

Part III

The old man knows this is all past,
and he will not have to wait long
for death.
He is dying now...
with each passing day,
he sits a while longer in his chair.
He knows the day will come
when he will be too exhausted
to raise himself for supper
or to manage one more breath.
Then attendants will press his eyelids closed
and he will be on his ways to Mildred.

Meanwhile, the old man survives
with his memories.
On stormy nights, he stands at the window
staring into the rain,
hoping lightning doesn't strike hi barn.

Miles away,
a shutter beat against the side
of a farmhouse,
the wind rises in the evergreens,
and a house stands vacant.

LET ME HELP

After the stones were cast,
after the lash was applied,
after the nails were driven,
Jesus died.

Give me a piece of his cloak,
give me a thorn from his crown,
tell me the words he spoke,
I'll help to write them down.

Let me help to roll the stone.
Let me fold his gown,
Or I can go find Peter,
does he know what Mary found?

Maybe, I could start a search
he could be nearby.
And I could speak to Thomas
as soon as he stops by.

Let me help.

KARLEEN

She survives in a corner of my memory,
vibrant, young, pretty,
with eyes that always looked
straight into mine.

I still see a little girl's pout
which disappears with each
uncontrollable smile.

Now she lay in a hospital bed.

When I entered the room,
she knew me from across the years
though I found it hard
to recognize her.

A woman's voice I did not know
greeted me: ordinary words
after fifteen years:
"How are you?"

God should now allow illness and years
to ravage youthful beauty
as fragile and precious as hers.

I bent over the side of the bed
and kissed her lips.
It was a dry kiss,
but my eyes were wet.

As kisses lacked passion.
But I always believed
dry lips and wet eyes
expressed more love
than the other way around.

Two tubes ran into the veins of her arm,
dripping manna from a plastic bag,
a modern science answer
to the Bible.

I was reminded of the tubes
in my brother's arm
when he was dying.
He was forty-five.
At forty-five, she might have time left.

She was working as a waitress
when I met her.
She was too young then
and I was too old,
so we became just friends.

Fate did not intend that we be lovers
though I believe she loved me,
and I loved her as much as
conscience would allow.

What's not meant to be, cannot be changed.

II

Tonight,
on a dance floor,
I watch a young woman
move to the beat of music.

She too is smiling, a lovely smile,
much like Karleen so long ago.
And I want to shout to her partner:
Stop! Focus! Click!

Capture this picture for your memory!

...where she will forever dance
on youthful legs.
lovely,
radiant,
and alive.

98

EDWARD REICH

Edward Reich
did not like
living in his town,
So he went to sea
where eventually
he drown.

The wife he sought
could not be taught
to satisfy his needs.

But now that Ed
is finally dead,
he solemnly concedes,

His life was always better
whenever he had let her
love him.

DILEMMA

I remember
hard as stone.
I remember
all alone.

I remember
cold and damp,
I thought the lady
was a tramp.

But now
that she has gone away
I must admit
I miss her.

If she comes back,
I'll get on-track,
I'll grab her
and I'll kiss her.

But if there is
an angry scene,
Undoubtedly,
that's sure to mean

I'll have to stop
dating her sister.

HOW THE WORLD CAN CHANGE

Little Jack Horner
can't find a corner.

Jack and Jill
can't find a hill.

A Jack named Sprat
eats only fat
(he's supposed to eat the lean).

And Cinderella
lost her fella
and when slipper didn't fit.

Little Bo Peep
did find her sheep
(but minus their tails behind them).

And Little Miss Muffet
told the spider to 'stuff it'!
Then stayed to finish her whey.

And Hansel and Gretel
will probably settle
for GPS someday.

So, if you're like Jack Horner
and can't find a corner,
at least give change a good try.

Just put in your thumb
and pull out a plum
and say, "What a good boy am I."

CALIFORNIA

I"ll always hate
the State of California
A forty-niner
I will never be.
For there's a woman
in the State of California,
and I wish that she were here
instead with me.

The San Fernando Valley
I won't sing about.
You will never hear me spout
kind words or praise
because there's a woman
that I love in California,
and Life and I,
we simply pass the days.

My heart will never lie
in San Francisco.
A pox on all the stars
in Hollywood.
How I wish that she would
come back to Wisconsin
where everything in life
had been so good.

Now the wines of Napa Valley,
I'll not drink no more.
They fail to inebriate
my head.
And there's a woman
who I pray each night
were here with me instead.

ELEGY FOR A BROTHER

I watched him die.
His last words
that I remember were
"I don't think I'm going to make it."

"Maybe not," I replied.

After that,
there may have been other words,
but not that I remember.

I wish now that I had said more,
but how was I to know
these were to be our last words?

The room was quiet
except for his breathing
and the pulsating sound
of a machine next to his bed.

Occasionally,
he coughed and spit sputum
into a steel dish.
But for the most part,
he looked as though he were asleep.

I sat alone with my thoughts
except when other family members
entered the room.

Then we talked in low voices
so as not to wake him.

His coma came in the afternoon.
We, who loved him,
gathered around his bed
as memories
of him overwhelmed us.

Afternoon passed into evening,
and visitors filtered in and out his room
— to pray, to visit, to talk of Larry.

We talk in quiet voices,
sometimes only in whispers
as we listened to his breathing.

Always the rasping
and gurgle of his breathing
intruded on the silence
in the room.

Occasionally,
a loud sigh escaped his throat,
raising alarm among us,

and suction would be used
to ease his breathing.

We all knew.
Hope was a lost cause.
Death would be soon.

Then let Death come!
What is there to fear?

"I am the Resurrection...
He who believes in Me will live forever!"

So go, Larry!
We know what awaits you us!

II

My sister Nancy and I
stayed the night keeping watch.
Everyone else had gone home to rest
and to wait for the telephone to ring.

The hospital was eerily quiet.
The hall was all but deserted.
Lights had been turned off or dimmed.

Near midnight,
we left the room
as nurses came to check his tubes
and to measure whatever life remained.

The clock outside his room
showed midnight when I noticed
the nurses were gone.

Intent on keeping my watch,
I returned.

The room was quiet.
He's resting peacefully, I thought.
No sound of strained breathing.

No sound of the machine pulsating.

Then I knew.

Larry lay too still.
His eyes were open,
fixed on the opposite-facing wall.

Holding back tears,
I went to get my sister.
"Larry's dead,"
I quietly announced.

As she comprehended the words,
her facial expression changed,
but she said nothing.

We returned to the room in silence,
She entering first,
I deferring to her.

And I thought of the Apostle John
who deferred to Peter at the Tomb.

Without a word or cry,
she bent to kiss our brother's forehead,
then lightly touched his lips with her hand.

That was her 'Goodbye',
her acceptance of his death –
and she left the room.

III

The last breathe.
The last heartbeat.
The last movement of a muscle.

The last brain wave
sent to travel the universe
to distant stars and planets.

And we are left behind.

HOMESICK

I stayed too long in Nashville.
It's to go back home.
Away from old surroundings,
I'm feeling quite alone.

Coffee at McDonald's,
wake up calls at 8:00,
Motel-6 ain't family,
Wisconsin, I can't wait.

I'm driving home tomorrow
along I-65,
and I'll drink a cold Milwaukee beer
as soon as I arrive.

ALL MY BERRIES

If my sweetheart ever marries,
all my berries
will be blue.

MY WISH

O' somewhere there is magic,
and somewhere there is rhyme,
wish I could buy a ticket
to somewhere back in time.

LINES I HAVE NOT USED
BUT THAT I LIKE

Love is like a candle,
it flares before it dies.

She said we were going nowhere,
but how did we arrive so soon?

I had the vim,
but I lacked the vinegar.

You threw away my heart,
so I picked it up
and I brought it back to you.

I have mountains to climb.
I am not going to worry
about the molehills you build.

It's like knocking on doors
to empty rooms.

The snap... crackle... and pop of gunfire.

She's a memory I left
in the smoke of the past.

Looking at myself
through rose-colored glasses;
I still don't like what I see.

Now that I drink alone,
I have no one with whom to differ.

He never met a man he did not like,
or a woman with a smile he did not love.

They had to amputate his soul.

Two words that I would like to rhyme:
dichotomy and lobotomy.

They rode the merry-go-round
of happenstance.

Sincerity is its own eloquence.

TIDBITS

WHAT SHE SAID

I told her:
You're an I-told-you-so kind of girl.

She said
No, I'm just your kind of girl

*GRa$FET¢Ti!

I saw your name on the chalkboard,
so I erased it with soap, water, vinegar,
alcohol, and Barkeeper's Friend.

I can't tolerate grafetti!

TO HELL WITH BASEBALL

Like a hundred-mile-an-hour fastball,
I never should have caught her smile.
O' God, how it hurt!

FRIDAY NIGHT SHEEPSHEAD
WITH THE BOYS

Like circled wagons
drawn together in need,
five men sit around
the sheepshead table,
holding their cards close.

Each player knows the rules:

queens take kings,
diamonds are trump,
you have to follow suit.

It's life on a smaller scale
you pay if you lose.

But they come together each month
seeking the Grail of friendship... and for fun.

Tom, you son-of -a-gun,
I got you now.

You're out of trump!
Frank, are you there?
You got the queen?

I'm here partner.
That trick gives us game.

Sorry, Harold.
I warned you not to pick
in front of me.

How'd you like those Black Ladies
in the blind?
Don't I take good care of you, Bert?

Have faith in me, Joe.
Would I give you stones to bury?
Hide your aces, Gentlemen.
There was nothing in the blind.

II

A litany of friendship and of fun.
celebrated with beer
and the incense of tobacco.

The day will come
when each of us will go
without a trick.

I hope it won't be
double on the bump.

And when it's time to settle
with the House,
I hope each has the chips
he started with.

Until then,
deal the cards again.

And this time
let's give Dick an ace,
so he can be a partner.

III

Now the table's empty
save for me.
I'll deal a final hand
to the empty chairs.

And I'll open up a can
of ice-cold bee,
then raising it,
I'll give a final cheer:

To all my friends
who spent their Friday nights
playing sheepshead with the boys.

TRAPPED

He gets along,
he marks the days,
a lab rat stuck
inside a maze.

Someone said,
"It's just a phase
he is going through."

But he feels trapped
like a frightened deer,
its reflection seen
in a broken mirror;

'and not like the sun'
in a morning haze,
but more like a horse
in a barn blaze

...he wants to leave,
but he stays.

ANIMAL CRACKERS

The Porcipine

The porcipine is mighty fine,
but he isn't any friend of mine.
If you see him lying in the road,
run over by a massive load,

beware!

even though his skin
shows pallor,
caution is the better part
of valor.

The Ardvaark

The ardvaark lives on juicy ants,
and immodestly, he wears no pants.
'Ants in his pants'
are not his passion,
which I think explains
his choice of fashion.

The Iguana

Bet you can't make
a rhyme for iguana.

Bet I could
If I wanna!

The Armadillo

The armadillo's quite a fellow,
but I think his brain is made of jello.
When I see him lying in the road,
run over by a heavy load,

I think, 'too b-a-a-d'!

Though he failed making it across
I hardly take that as a loss.
To me it isn't a surprise
that crossing roads spelled his demise.

007

Hang onto your neck brace.
Grab hold of your heart.
Cling tight to the dashboard,
she's learning to park.

Call your insurance man.
MAKE OUT YOUR WILL.
If she passes the test,
she'll be licensed to kill.

IMMIGRANT

A chink named Wong
from a Chinese tong
who spoke sing-song
pronounced it wrong.

Someone shouted out at him:
"If you say it wrong,
\you don't belong."
So be gone
Wong!

Say: bye-bye

IT'S PRIVATE

I can't recite my love upon a stage
for public eyes and ears to tread upon.

Like Cordelia to her father, I resist
the public demonstration of affection.

For love is not a thing to be paraded,
but something kept at home for private viewing.

PROOF

When love ends, it can break your heart,
and I have the pieces to prove it.

WE WERE CATERPILLARS

Like caterpillars,
we had lived five years
in the darkness of our cocoon.

Now metamorphosis is slowly
changing our friendship
into a higher form intimacy.

We need to think.
Do we want our friendship
to emerge as a marriage?

...two butterflies
taking flight together
in the sun?

THOUGHTS WHILE TRAVELING ON A TRAIN COMING BACK FROM CALIFORNIA

The year is 2012.

I'm riding on a train back from California,
sitting in the lounge car alone.
It's late at night and all the other passengers
have retired to their coach cars.
Me? I'm looking out the window at the passing night.

Occasional lights appear in the darkness
sometimes miles in the distance.
Trucks are passing on lonely highways,
outlined by the orange and red lights of their trailers
that give shape to silhouettes of black.

I think of the men who drive theses trucks
-- what life do they have on the road,
away from home and family – alone,
days at a time, except for brief smiles
at truck stops?

I see lone ranches and occasional towns
I will never visit.
The lights of the houses are mostly isolated
by the surrounding darkness of night

though sometimes the houses are clustered
in two's, three's or as many as five.

The changing night scenery outside the windows
reminds me of the changing scenes of my life,
and the people who disappeared from it
as I transitioned from boy to a man of middle-age.

I think of Shakespeare's words
that we are all actors who strut upon a stage
and then are seen no more.

Such is our human existence.

II

I decide to go to my seat in the coach car
to see if Mary Ann wants to sit up with me.
The lounge car is empty at this late hour,
so we would have it to ourselves.
But she is asleep in her seat,
and I decide not to wake her.

Probably better to be alone with my thoughts.

I return to the lounge car
and resume my seat at the window.
Nothing has changed outside in the darkness
but now my thoughts have changed,
and memory has taken over

... and I remember 1985,
another time that I had returned from California.
I am thinking of Sylvia who had stayed behind in 1985.
She is dead now – I learned of her death some years ago.

I had met Sylvia by accident in the winter of 1985.
I was minding my business at the RED MILL,
a jazz bar in Waukesha County where I lived.
I was listening to the music.

She later told me that she had picked me
from among the men in the bar
to show her girl friend how to meet men.
Instead, our meeting and conversation
led to a date the following week.

We agreed to see the movie "White Knights"
which starred the Russian ballet master,
Mikhail Baryshnikov, and the American dancer
Gregg Hines.

The night of our date was cold,
and afterward I took Sylvia directly home.
I was waiting for her to enter the house
and turn on the lights before driving off
when she knocked on my car window.
-- she didn't have her house keys!

After giving the problem some thought,
I suggested breaking the window.
I walked around the house like a burglar
looking for an easy entry,
finally deciding to break a pane of glass
on the patio door. Success!

Grateful, she invited me in to warm up
before driving home – and so it began.

III

The train's whistle blows mournful warnings
at dark crossings.
It glides on its tracks so smoothly
that I cannot tell if we are moving
except for the lights the window
that appear and disappear in the night.

As I stare out the window into darkness,
it isn't hard for me to remember 1985,
for the time we had was short-lived
-- Sylvia was moving to California.
Her parents lived there and she had a job
waiting for her at the hospital in Loma Linda.

In the weeks we had together,
I helped her pack for the movers.
I saw her off on the final day,
and I held her hand
when the mover's truck pulled away.

I followed her car to the park-and-ride lot
where we would say our goodbyes.
She made me promise I would come visit her
that summer when she was settled.
Then she got into the car.

I watched her car drive away
until it disappeared in the distance.
I don't know how long I sat there,
not knowing where to go or what to do.
I didn't care.

That night she called me from a motel
to let me know she was safe and where she was.
She was tired and lonely,
and wished I was there.
After reminding me of my promise,
she said good night.

IV

I kept my promise.
After school ended for the summer,
I left for California in June,
on the pretext of taking a summer class
at Chapman College in Orange.

I stayed with Sylvia in Redlands
for more than a week,
attending classes daily at Chapman,
while she went to her job at the hospital
in nearby Loma Linda.

Our time together was joyous,
We went to the Redlands Bowl,
Lake Arrowhead in the San Bernadino
Mountains, and to Palm Springs
where we rode up to the sky in a tram

-- to the top of the San Jacinto Mountain,
10,834 feet above the world.

But time was our enemy.
We both knew that my visit would end,
and I would be returning 'home'
when the class ended at Chapman.

Sadness is a part of life.
I left two days after the class ended
and this time no promises were made.

V

The train is slowing,
for I am watching a truck on the highway pass us.
The highway and our tracks
have been following the same route
for much of the night as we travel east.

As we near our stop in Salt Lake City,
there are more lights and buildings now.
I see a great building to the north,
in glorious light, illuminating the night sky
~~ it stands as a beacon to the lost.

In spite of the late hour,
people are waiting the train's arrival.
I think about going into the station
for a look around, but am hesitant
for fear of the train leaving without me.

Instead, I watch the people on the platform
load their luggage.

The stop seems to be lasting a long time
~~ I estimate thirty minutes.
Finally, the train begins to move,
and I check my watch—4:33 AM,
not long before sunrise.

I think it is time to wake Mary Ann,
for we will soon be entering the mountains,
and it should be a beautiful day.

JEFFERY D.

I told her:

Jeffery D.
is in the slammer.

Someone ought to
take a hammer,
smash his teeth,
and end his stammer.

'Then, change the locks,'
'and guard the walls,'
watch him in
the bathroom stalls.

Check his mail
and search his cell.
Make his life
a living Hell!

The murdering cuss,
why make a fuss
if he should die?

Deny him hope,
let him kiss the rope.

...bye bye!

FOR YET MORE STORMS

Like a nugget
you found prospecting,
I am assayed to determine my worth.

Skeptically, I am weighed
against other nuggets
you have found.

If my assessment score is low,
will you toss me aside
to lie and wait
until other prospectors claim me?

Is my value
to be determined
only by calculation
of the gold or silver
that can be gleaned
from melting me down
in the crucible of your experience?

I am not a vault
that contains riches
beyond dream.
I am only a nugget
you stumbled on by chance
when you were trudging up a mountain.

But, consider me.
Caress me in your hands,
clasp me in your hands,
clasp me to your heart,
gaze at me with honest eye.

Then, scan the horizon
that lies beyond
where you now stand
in your search for happiness.

Maybe
I can lead you
to the mother lode you seek,
buried in life's mountains.

But I ask
not to be put back
for yet more storms
to tumble and erode me

until I am nothing.

IN THE MIDNIGHT HOUR

I sat on the bed in my motel
listening for your call.
The sound of a TV playing
was coming through the wall.

The red light wasn't flashing,
the telephone was still.
I waited in the darkness,
no message from you still.

In the midnight hour, I miss you.
In the midnight hour, I ache.
That hour is the loneliest,
that's when my heart breaks.

II

The motel clock, it must have stopped
since I last looked at it.
Bathroom faucet's dripping,
Time doesn't mind a bit.

I'll leave this room when morning comes,
and the sun knocks on my door.
I'll leave behind a pile of dreams
scattered on the floor.

In the midnight hour, I miss you

but it's after midnight now,
and this longing that I have for you
won't leave me anyhow.

I ASKED SANTA

I asked Santa to bring me Nancy.
She's the girl that I fancy.
Put her on that open sleigh,
and bring her to me Christmas Day.

I tell you Santa, I'm so romance-y
Here I sit without my Nancy.
I can't even trim the tree
if you don't end this misery.

I won't make you use the chimney
if it's Nancy that bring me.
Just fill my stocking with her charms,
and put her in my empty arms.

But listen, Santa, can't you hurry?
You always fill my mind with worry.
I'm afraid that time is fleeting,
we could miss our annual meeting.

So can you move it, slowpoke, skip your greeting
to all the folk you chance on meeting.
Get those reindeer in high gear;
don't make me wait until next year.
And remember, Santa, fill my fancy,
and on Christmas, bring me Nancy.

She'll provide my Christmas cheer,
so you can skip my house net year.

JANET

Like the sun at dawn
When all of Earth is seen
before it,
her smile chases darkness
from my world.

And even when clouds fill my sky,
her smile still shines brightly
above my Earth,
emitting rays of love
that warmed a heart

that might have grown cold

MY SON TALKS TO ME NOW

My son talks to me now.
Only a few words like 'horse' or 'cow'.
Or when my wife asks: "Where is Daddy?" He answers, 'School.'

He is growing up, and I am feeling old. I am only twenty-one, the age at which one supposedly passes into adulthood; yet, it will not be long before I am forty-one, fifty-one, or seventy-one.

Then dead.

Lately, I notice that I am always trying to cling to the past, hoping to make the present stand still and the future keep its distance.

Needless to say, I do not succeed.
Time, in fact, seems to pass more rapidly, for in clinging to the past, I am all the more aware that something happened a year ago, rather than a month or week ago.

My life is hurriedly rushing to its end which I can in no way impede. It is gaining momentum, and I expect a tremendous crash followed by silence, in which the end will come as Eliot said— "not with a bang, but a whimper."

Having thought of death, my hope is that I should die in spring, not in the midst of a hot summer, nor in autumn, nor in winter. Winter is the death of a year—cold, lifeless, snow-shrouded. The brown stubble of the fields braced against the wind indicates life that is past.

Therefore, I choose spring in which to die, for in spring, life is rejoicing everywhere, and I would rather leave life in a joyous time when the lilacs and pear blossoms are in their splendor. These blooms have no connotation of death, only of birth and new life.

So spring is altogether a good time in which to die, for then the hope of a new year lies ahead, and the positive force of life is active—the old is being replaced by the new as I am being replaced by my son

...who as I said: talks to me now.

GEORGE THE GREEK

We called him "George the Greek" or "Old George," and we laughed at his inability to speak English. But George was wise in his years, and in his day had been quite the 'romantic.'

He was still handsome at seventy; his hair had merely turned to gray. Small in build, George was strong and his muscles had turned to iron with age. He dressed well, always wearing a suit and tie, and everything that he possessed had the quality of character and selection.

It was common knowledge that he carried several hundred dollars on his person. No one knew, however, how he had ever acquired so much money though it was rumor that in his earlier days George had been a gambler.

A particular mystery to everyone was the diamond engagement ring that he wore on the small finger of his left hand. Evidently, he attached sentimental value to it, although it could not have been worth more than a couple of hundred dollars.

It was conjecture that the ring once belonged to a girl whom George had loved. However, nothing was known of the girl—whether she had died or had rejected him—and George never said anything that enlightened us though we believed that he loved her deeply, for he never married, and he never removed the ring.

In his later years, George helped in a restaurant just to have something to do. He had no known relatives and few real friends though he was acquainted with nearly everyone.

Having no one close, George spent the time between the restaurant and his room, at the movies, or sitting in the bus terminal.

However, what he liked most to do was to talk of Greece when he was young, for Greece once had a glorious past, and evidently, George once had one too.

A WEDDING TOAST

Welcome, friends and relatives of Larry and Jolane. I'm Bob Hoskins, the groom's uncle and godfather.

Larry's mother Beverly asked if I would act on behalf of my nephew, Michael, to present a toast to the bride and groom. It seems that Mike is still a little shy about standing up in public and addressing a crowd, so I have the honor of toasting the new couple.

However, I cannot let the occasion pass without first making reference to the one person we all wish could have lived to see this day—Larry's father, Lawrence Sr. It sounds funny to refer to Larry as senior. He would have been proud of his son and daughter-in-law on this day. And he would have been happy. For Larry Senior loved to attend weddings. He loved to dance to polkas and dances; he loved to drink the beer, to eat the food, and to kiss the brides.

In other words, he loved to have fun—and isn't that why we come, for the fun to be had by everyone? Because weddings are happy occasions. They are an opportunity to get together with family and friends when too often our individual lives keep us apart.

And while we miss Larry Senior, he would not want us to be sad on this day. He would want us to celebrate... to give young Larry and Jolane a good send-off on their life together as man and wife.

Larry and Jolane, this day is a happy day for you. You will remember it always until the day you die. And I'm sure you know there will be unhappy days for you too, probably days of anger and regret.

But the picture isn't dark, because let me tell you that statistically you will both live longer, suffer less illness, and be happier than people who do not marry. This is only statistically, but the reason is that you have someone with whom you can share and lean on for emotional support. Marriage is a healthy lifestyle and I recommend it.

From my experience, however, there will be one great disadvantage—you will be a lot poorer. Maybe two can live as cheaply as one, but certainly not three, four, or five. And when the children come, so will be the bills. Take my word for it,the bills will never stop coming. Your grandparents will verify this truth.

Larry and Jolane, from this day on, you will have to compromise with each other; you will have to share with each other; you will have to sacrifice for each other; and you will have to forgive each other.

But, if you do these things, you will be rewarded; you will reap dividends of happiness that wealth cannot buy.

Remember this day, keep it holy, and let God be a part of your lives. So with this advice, I and all here present offer this toast to you... Michael, finish what I started.

[Michael] To my brother and his wife... may they love each other always.

SPEECH AT THE LADY PITTS RECOGNITION DAY PROGRAM

LADY PITTS CENTER, JUNE 8, 1992

Before I announce the names of the students that I have selected for awards, I have an official announcement.

Some of you have heard that I am retiring from teaching. Today, I am making the announcement official. Next week is my last week, and I am retiring after 33 years.

Standing here today, thirty-three years is not a long time because it seems like only yesterday that I faced my first students at Oconomowoc High School.

It was an auditorium muck like this, and it was freshman orientation, the first days of September. John F. Kennedy was President.

Since then, I have tried to make the world better. I ask you students to do the same: make this world a better place. You know where to start. Start with yourselves.

Be better persons in your homes, in your school, in your community. Study! Get an education! Read! Learn about everything!

Make your stay at Lady Pitts the watershed of your life. Build on your days spent here so that you have a chance to accomplish your dreams.

Someday, some of you in this room will be traveling in space. Wherever you go in this universe, take good with you.

Only four years of my life have I been at Lady Pitts—four very happy years.
The girls that I had in my classes have been wonderful. I would be
proud to have many of you as my daughters. I love you very much.

My own daughter Elizabeth, when she was 16, had a baby. She was a junior
in high school. After her son was born, she stayed in school, and the next
year she was graduated. You can do the same.

I have selected two students for wards. They represent many of the fine
students I had this year as well as in the past.

One in middle school student that I have had in social studies for the whole
year. The other is a high school student that I had in U.S. History the whole
year.

Both students have worked hard all year doing A and B work. Both students
had simply excellent attendance in my class. Both students have been a joy.
At this time, I ask Sonya Rogers and Bertha Whitelow to come forward.

(Awards given to students. Read inscriptions on music boxes: "You are free
to conquer the world.")

Well, what do I have for the rest of you students? Something... at least for
many of you.

Today, I have signed a decree—hear our vocabulary word <u>decree</u>. English
students? Today, I have signed a decree that all debts owed to me by the
students of Lady Pitts are hereby forgiven. These debts are legally canceled,
and I will burn your IOU's along with all my tests.

Finally, I cannot leave without saying how proud I am to have served with
the faculty and staff at Lady Pitts. A finer group of people doest not exist
anywhere. They care about you students; they want you to succeed.
And, if they get on you, if they push you to come to school and study, if they

correct your inappropriate behavior or talk, it is because they want you to succeed and to have a good life.

My final words to the students are these: Read! Read! Read! All the great people in history have been readers. The greatest Presidents of our country have been readers and have read hundreds and hundreds of books:

Thomas Jefferson
James Madison
Abraham Lincoln
Franklin Roosevelt
Harry Truman
John F. Kennedy

All were readers, and I am sure that Martin Luther King Jr. was a great reader as well, because as a minister, he read the greatest of all books—the Bible.

How are you ever going to be a thinker if you don't read? How will you ever know the thoughts, the beliefs, the ideas, and the hopes of great people if you don't read?

What are you going to do to learn what they have learned before you were born? Are you going to go to the cemetery and talk to the dead?

The only way to learn from the great people of the past is to read their words. And you find their words in books. Treasure books!

And my last words to you are to repeat the words I had inscribed on the music boxes: "You are free to conquer the world."

Go out and conquer it!

FAREWELL SPEECH

LEAVING OCONOMOWOC HIGH SCHOOL

I should have bought my American Express card with me this morning because a lot of you might be wondering who I am. It's been so long now—two years since I left!

I asked if I could have a phone booth up here so I could step inside to change like Clark Kent. You all knew who emerged from the phone booth—a guy with a big letter S on his shirt!

Well! since there isn't a phone booth handy, the metamorphosis will have to take place in the open. I just have to change from Bob Hoskins into—THE ROCK! (take off shirt)

For those in the back of the room who can't see my shirt, it doesn't have an 's' on the chest. The shirt says: "I survived Cooney High School!"

Even Superman would have trouble doing that!

Some of you may not know this, but this is the second time that I am leaving Oconomowoc. The first time was in 1974 when I left to become the Executive Secretary of the State Bingo Control Board.

Ah, yes, my second time. It is not the same as the first. When I left in 1974, Oconomowoc High School was a different place than it is today. That was about the time that Ray Hornig left education to become an administrator. I do not know what John Koehn was doing then, but I think it was something useful.

When I left in 1974, Oconomowoc had a Men's Breakfast for retiring teachers, not a midnight snack in the dark of night. This event now starts so early that after closing up the bars in Milwaukee last night, I hurried right out here so I wouldn't be late.

COULD SOMEONE PLEASE CHECK TO SEE IF I LEFT MY CAR LIGHTS ON!

As I said, this is my second time to leave Oconomowoc, and to be honest, this time it's different for me. I know it is tradition for teachers who are leaving to poke fun at the administration, but that's a tradition I never approved of. So at the risk of disappointing many of my old co-workers, I am not going to say anything against Hornig, Rickabaugh, or Koehn, except to say that I see the three stooges are in the room this morning.

Truthfully, though, I do miss the good old days when administrators came with thick skins, instead of thick heads.

Let me begin by telling you what I have been doing these last two years. I teach at a school in the Milwaukee system called Lady Pitts. It's located in the old Lincoln High School, three blocks from Lake Michigan.

Lady Pitts is a school for teenage parents. The students are all girls who are either pregnant or who have had a child in the past year. We start classes at 8:15 in the morning and dismiss at 3:10 in the afternoon, my kind of hours.

The girls I teach are wonderful, lovely, and highly motivated to learn, and more than 75% are black. It has been a long time since I have had students like them. I would be proud to have most of them for my daughters.

Most of the girls realize that Lady Pitts is an opportunity for them to graduate. And many of them hold onto the dream that they are going to go to college or other schooling.

Sadly, for many of them, this ambition will probably remain a dream. We have one girl in middle school who was back this year and gave birth to her second child.

How will her dream ever come true?

But I love the students, and I love my fellow teachers, and I love what I am doing. I am happy.

Additionally, I was elected building representative for our union, and I have represented the school at three Milwaukee School Board meetings to maintain support for our program.

All kidding aside, I want to publicly thank John Koehn ad Jim Rickabaugh. I want to thank them for the opportunity they gave me to take a year's leave from Oconomowoc to see if I could find greener pastures.

Well, I found a greener pasture, a job that I love, and I will be forever grateful to both these gentlemen for the opportunity to explore. I truly appreciate that, and I thank them.

So now I am leaving for my second and last time. But this time, it really isn't the same as 1974. That day I drove home with tears streaming down my face—not today.

Back in 1974, I use to have my classes read a poem titled 'Where Are You Now, Batman.' It was about all our heroes having gone away.

Now all my heroes are gone. The giants who held the Hill so many years before my arrival are gone – either in retirement or their final resting places.

Names from the past that I carry with me—names that live on in the beliefs and in the souls of those they taught.

Rudy Timmel
Bill Ohm
Chuck Hocking
Corbin Stanelle
Les Leschensky
Bob Erickson
Bill Martin
Curt Winter
Ernie Nicolette
Gene Iffland
John Koehler
Wally Reams
Lud Kroner
Joe St. Thomas

And lest I be accused of being a sexist:

Mary Hughes
Bertha Hodgson
Mary Baird
and Dorothy Babcock

All of them were here when I came. Now, they are all gone. They are unsung heroes, but today, I sing their names to you.

Only one of my heroes is still going strong. Lyman Humphrey. And I saw him here today. Lyman, I want you to know that I forgive you. I forgive you for going into the faculty room on a Sunday to put in your entry for the football pool.

I would have done the same thing, Lyman, but the Administration never gave me a key to the building. So alas, though it is true that some things have changed since 1974, some things will never change.
To conclude, I will add the name of a past giant that some may not

remember, or may not have known: Dave Pritzlaff.

Dave Pritzlaff walked the halls of Oconomowoc High School on crutches. He taught social studies, and my sister was one of his students. You see, Dave needed crutches because one of his legs was blown off in World War II, but his service did not end in post-war America. He became a teacher.

For me, reading these name this morning is like reading the names on a war memorial in the local park. Maybe communities should erect similar memorials for teachers who serve so long.

After today, my name will join the list, and I like to think that I fought the good fight, that I served with some distinction, and that I belong up there with the others.

In my going, I leave the field to others still serving. I leave it to you in this room, most of you whom I have known and worked with for many years:

Tom Pinter
Chuck Thorsen
Joe Unrein
Carl Duch
Dick Whalen
Bob Harrold
John Kleinschmidt
Bob Wilson
Lee Fenzel

and to the granddaddies who still stand tall:

Jim Fuller
and
Dave Smith

I have enjoyed my stay with you and I leave content. All of you are in my heart and in my memories, and there you will stay until I die, which I hope

will not be for a long time.
I end with the words that Jesus spoke to His disciples:

"Peace Be With You!
My Peace I Leave You!"

REMARKS AT INDUCTION TO PALMYRA-EAGLE ALUMNI HALL OF FAME

I am here today to pay tribute. Not to the honorees to the Wall of Fame, but to the people of Palmyra-Eagle who supported them.

My name is Bob Hoskins—Robert more formally—Class of 1953. I was born in Milwaukee, WI, but after my dad died when I was eight years old, my mother married a farmer and milk hauler named Gib Wendt. He was a good man, and I became a farm boy like so many of my classmates at Palmyra.

I went to Maple Grove, a one-room country school with about 26 other kids in eight grades. Ida Baneck was my teacher for sixth, seventh, and eighth grade, and Darlene Lucht was my only classmate in those grades.

Later, Darlene and I attended Palmyra High School together, but I have not seen her since graduation in 1953 though I have seen others in her family occasionally through the years.

My brother Larry and a neighbor-girl Janet Strike (whom I married) were a year behind me (in Danny Poulson's class), and my brother-in-law, Roger Strike, was a year ahead of me.

My younger sister, Nancy and Kathy Hoskins, lived for a year with the Jack and Agnes Hooper family near Zion. As foster children, they joined the Jefferson County Sanitorium for two years. Their son, John Hooper, was in my brother's class.

Other good neighbors were Guy and Rose Boos, Glen and Leona Strike, and Orley and Marge Gilbert.

Our neighbor, Mary Ebbott, was our 4-H leader, and Jack Mill was the 4-H nemesis of my brother Larry and me. You see, Jack Mill, Larry, and I were the only exhibitors one year at the Jefferson Co. Fair showing Brown Swiss cattle. Unfortunately, we had a judge who was ignorant and blind in one eye. Jack was awarded the blue ribbon, and my brother and I were each awarded red ribbons for second place.

If Jack were alive, he might not even remember this miscarriage of justice, but I still remember. That judge probably could not tell a Brown Swiss from a Jersey.

Why do I mention this personal history? I mention it because these are some of the hundreds of people from Palmyra area in Jefferson County who influenced me to become what I turned out to be: a teacher and a citizen-politician.

From somewhere in the milieu that I described, I received the motivation to do the right things in life that I valued and that I thought needed doing, and I am
sure the name is true of my fellow honorees.

One-room country schools, Palmyra High School with its fire escape and six-man football team—no television, no computers.

Yet, I tell people proudly that out of my senior class of 34 students, two of my classmates have taught at Harvard University. If I am mistaken about this, please don't tell me. I want to continue believing that it's true.
The buildings in which children learn and the equipment that goes in them provide children with advantages to learn.

But to blossom in life, children need the inspiration that I was given:
  • they need dreams;

- they need parents and teachers with virtue, who provide love and direction;
- they need classmates who provide companionship, moral support, and friendship;
- and they need the world of books that expose them to ideas, history, science, literature, and the biographies of people who dreamed their dreams and fought good fights.

After a lifetime, I can recite the names of my teachers: Phil Nelson and Bob Schuh, Ed Geese and Jerome Brecht, Jean Carmody and George Nelson. Though I did not have George Nelson as a teacher, he help create the environment with the others.

They were all a part of this wonderful place in the world where I lived and went to school.

They were people who loved us and helped us; who inspired us and guided us; who befriended us and taught us; and who made us who we are. So my thanks to the people of Palmyra-Eagle, past and present, for what I became and for the life I have lived.

Speaking for myself, I am beholden to the people of Palmyra-Eagle for the life I have lived

We rise on the sacrifice of others.

POLITICAL SPEECH 1968

CAMPAIGN FOR STATE ASSEMBLY

As a candidate for public office, I have been told: "Don't speak on welfare needs. The welfare budget is too big, and voters are tired of seeing welfare money going to people too lazy to work."

Well, maybe what I say won't change anyone's mind. But I want to speak on welfare issues anyway because I think candidates must be honest with the voters and inform them where the candidate stands on issues. I do not intend to hide my views under any political blanket.

I know taxes are high. I pay $500 property taxes on a $15,500 home. Many of you pay more where you live. But do you know what the State of Wisconsin will spend on so-called welfare in the 1967-71 biennial budget-$389,700,000!

Sounds like a lot of money, doesn't it?

Well, it is a lot of money! But first remember that the appropriation is not for one year, but for two!

Furthermore, did you know that out of all that money, only $37,800,000—less than 10%—is spent on welfare as we think of it. The rest is spent for mental health, public health, and correctional institutions like Waupon State Prison, the Green Bay Reformatory, the Wales and Plymouth Schools for Boys, and the School for Girls at Oregon.

The Medical program for the elderly is included in the appropriation. Eliminate all these other programs, and the welfare budget for two years is not nearly so much as people criticize it for.

In Wisconsin, the per capita average spent on ADC (Aid to Dependent Children) is $7.55. This is below the national average of $12.40.

An average family of four on welfare in Wisconsin receives $2,600 a year. This is $1,000 less than the federally defined poverty level—rent included. In addition, the family can qualify for $45 of surplus food. This is for a family of four—and this is what some uninformed people all "luxury".

Let's explode some myths about public welfare: Do you believe people are poor because they have so many children? The average number of children is 2.8. That is not a large family by any standard.

Do you think that people on welfare make it a way of life once they get on welfare? The average ADC recipient in Wisconsin received aid for 15 months; the national average is two years. Does that sound like a lifetime on welfare?

Next, do you think the amount of state taxes for public assistance is sky rocketing? The dollar cost, it is true, has gone up, but not in relation to the state budget!

As a percentage of the executive budget, the amount for public assistance has decreased from 34% of the budget in 1955 to 24% in 1968!

Finally, do you think we should put welfare mothers to work? Good, I say! But will they get hired? What are their chances in today's job market? What are their skills?

You hear slogans: "Hire the handicapped." Most welfare mothers are educationally handicapped. Did you know that 66% of the mothers on ADC did not complete high school, and 33% did not complete eight grade? With these qualifications, what are their chances of finding jobs that will take them of welfare? Even at this, 10% of these mothers are employed besides raising their children.

You see, what happens in all the myths about welfare is this: somebody knows of a case that he thinks is not deserving of assistance, and from this, he generalizes that many on welfare are undeserving.

But ladies and gentlemen, there is little fraud. I was a caseworker for Waukesha County Welfare Dept. two years, and I did not encounter one chiseler. I saw the needy—the blind, disabled, aged, and dependent children. One last point I should make: ADC mothers receive 21¢ per person for each meal. Governor Knowles, God bless him, recommended that this amount be increased to 26¢ per meal. Knowles' intentions were good, but intentions are not enough.

Knowles was afraid to knock heads with Representatives Shabaz, Merkle, and Froelich in the Assembly. As a result, they won the welfare budget issues, and Knowles lost. Meal assistance for recipients stayed at 21¢ per meal.

The next time you hear anyone speaking about the luxury of living on welfare, would you do this? If the man has a wife and two children, reach in your pocket and dig out 84 cents. Tell him to give it to his wife, and tell her to make dinner for the family!

Then when they say grace at the meal, they can also give thanks that, but for the Grace of God, go themselves every night of the week.

Thank you for coming, and thank you for listening.

AND DON'T FORGET TO VOTE!

SPEECH AT THE 45th REUNION OF OCONOMOWOC

HIGH SCHOOL CLASS OF 1965

September 5, 2010

Hello Class of 1965!

I want to take some time, first to attend to some business. I have some papers I need to return to some students from January 1961, so if they are here, will they come forward to pick up their work. (Names are read and papers are returned.)

With business taken care of, as long as I have the microphone, I'll say a few things.

First, I had every intention of being here five years ago, but it became a sad and tragic day. I was literally ready to walk out the door when the phone rang.

Mary Ann answered it, and then I heard her scream.
I ran into the room where she was sobbing.
Her grandson had died in Afghanistan.

His name was Ryan Nass, and he had turned 21 YEARS OLD five days earlier.
I had been his mentor at the National Guard Academy at Fort McCoy.

Obviously, we could not come that day and bring our sadness to your happy occasion. But life has to go on, and time heals wounds. This weekend we are here to celebrate with you.

The papers I brought from 50 years ago, are not the only thing I bring tonight. I bring a birthday card from October 1962. It's homemade and signed by many, many, many of you in the Class of 1965. It was my 27th birthday.

I always heard it was started by Randy Pesicek, but if anyone knows differently, let me know,
since Randy denies it. (Hold up card and open it.)

The card reads:
"TO ROCK, A GENTLEMAN AND A SCHOLAR"
Happy Birthday – and that is no lie,
from the students to Cooney High.
We like you Rock, and all your kin;
and hope someday you'll be an Assemblyman.
Well, we'll see you at the polls,
Signed—the students on the Honor Rolls

You have no idea how I cherish this old piece of cardboard.
I've kept it all these years, and whenever I read your names,
I see you as you were then: young and vibrant; just kids.

The members of the Class of 1965 will forever be kids in my memory. You may think you are old when you look in the mirror, and you see gray hair, lost hair, dimmer eyesight, and aching joints.
(Some of you may even be collecting social security.)

But, you should see yourselves in my mirror:
you are all young, still kids, with life ahead of you.

I have been thinking this weekend that when I die,

I will have this card and these names buried with me.
I'll take it to my grave with my life memories.

Because I tell you truly, I always thought the Class of '65
was the finest class of students to go through Oconomowoc
High School in my time. Incidentally, I told this to Chuck Thorson some
years ago, and he agreed.

But, don't fool yourselves that you can now rest on your laurels;
that you are ready to lie in a hammock; or play with your grandkids.
There are lots of things in your lives that are still waiting
for you to get busy on.

I do not know what they are—you may not know what they are—
but believe me, the tasks of life are out there.
It is up to you to go find them.

I looked for a magazine article this morning that I had laying around for a
year or more, but I couldn't find it.

Anyway, it was about the great books, the great discoveries of science, the
inventions, the works of art, and other accomplishments by people AFTER
THE AGE OF 60. I think Winston Churchill became Prime Minister of
Great Britain around age 70 when World War II brought him out of
retirement.

So, for your homework, all of you are to continue working on the projects
currently in your life, or start new ones. Many of you have done a good job
so far in making your small piece of world better, but remember, the job
is not finished, and neither are you at your ages.

So, if I do not see you again, let this be my goodbye; otherwise, we will talk
again down the road.

Until then, may God's blessing be upon you.
Hopefully, I will see you in five years.

COMMENCEMENT AND RECOGNITION DAY AT LADY PITTS (JUNE 3, 1994)

GOOD AFTERNOON to all my old friends here at Lady Pitts, to you students, guests, and especially to those being honored and who are graduating. My name is Bob Hoskins, and I taught here before retiring.

I, myself, am honored, very honored, to be here speaking today. I come to speak to you about yourselves and you futures.

Each and every one of you can be someone great or someone of good character. By great, I don't mean the whole world will know of you. I mean you can be someone great in your community, in your church, at the place where you work, or in the circle of your friends.

Each and every one of you can accomplish goals tomorrow that are only dream today. But IT'S ALL UP TO YOU. You are going to hear me say that a lot today – IT'S ALL UP TO YOU!

It isn't going to be up to your parents or other family members although they may help. It isn't going to be up to the State of Wisconsin or the federal government. Again, they may help. But it will be up to you.

Now, some of you may be wondering—how successful is this guy? What does he know about how to become successful? Well, I'm not going to tell you about my success in life, whatever they have been.

But in a few minutes, I'm going to tell you about my failures, not my successes. You see, in spite of failures in life, you can still be measured a success.

Booker T. Washington said:
"Success is measured, not so much by the position that one reaches in life, as by the obstacles that a person overcomes while trying to succeed."

I'll repeat that: (Read quotation again.)
Now, that makes me feel good—we measure success by the obstacle we overcome. I had lots of obstacles in my life, and I'm going to tell you some of them:

- not because I want you to admire me,
- not because I want to impress you,
- but because I know that many of you have big obstacles too. I want you to tell yourself—if he can be successful, so can I!

Here are some obstacles from my life:

I spent the first ten years of my life living at 1822 W. Walnut Street in Milwaukee – and then my father died of Hodgkins Disease (a type of cancer). I don't know how old he was when he died, but he was about 30.

My mother was left with four children: my brother and me, and two baby sisters. My mother cleaned the tavern on the corner of 19th Walnut, which was still there the last time I drove by.

About a year and a half after my father died, my mother married a farmer and we moved out of Milwaukee.

Five years later, when I was a freshmen in high school, my mother almost died. She spent over two years in a TB hospital, and we couldn't see her because tuberculosis was a dreaded, contagious disease, and children were

not permitted in the hospital.
The first year my mother was gone, our family stayed together. My brother
who was 13 years old, did the cooking and baking—including Thanksgiving
and Christmas dinners.

The second year, my sisters went to a foster home, and my brother and I
went to a Catholic seminary where we lived with 35-40 other boys.

After graduation from high school, I attended Carroll College in Waukesha,
Wisconsin. When I started college, I had maybe a dollar in my pocket. The
first day at Carroll. I borrowed $25 from an emergency fund in the Dean's
Office, and I used the money to buy my textbooks.

Four years later, I left Carroll with a degree. In between, I studied and
worked. One semester I slept on a couch and in my car. I didn't have a room.
Another semester I got up at 3:30 in the morning, three days a week, to meet
the mail trains at 4:00 and 6:oo am. After eating breakfast at 7:00 am I went
to classes and studied until noon.

At noon, I worked an hour in a restaurant and was paid a meal—no money.
Back to school all afternoon.

At supper time, back to the restaurant to work for my meal. Then, I went to
a bowling alley to set pins until 10:00 pm three nights a week. Study until
midnight every night and start over.

Was it easy? No!
Was I happy? Yes!
because I had a goal, and I was making progress toward it.

If you want something, go work for it! It's all up to you. As Booker T.
Washington said: We measure success by the obstacles we overcome.
Now, I want to tell you that throughout my life, I ave also known failure—

failure to reach goals I really, really wanted. And I even wondered why God had me do things If I were supposed to fail at them. Maybe God wanted me to learn failure.

While I was in college, a dream had begun to grow in me. I wanted to be a senator or a congressman in our government so I could help people like my

family who were poor. I wanted to make this world a better place.
So, how do you get to be a senator or congressman? You begin by running for public office. I started in 1962.

In 1962, a friend of mine was working for the Governor. He asked me if I would help the Democratic Party by running for the State Assembly in Waukesha County, a very Republican county.

- I ran and I lost.
- In 1964, my same friend was running for Congress, and I was asked to help the county ticket. I ran for Register of Deeds and I lost.

In 1966, I ran for the State Senate and lost.

- In 1970, I ran for the State Assembly and lost.
- In 1972, I ran for the State Senate—again because a candidate was needed—and I lost.
- In 1981, I ran for the State Senate in a special election and I lost.
- And in 1982, I ran for the State Assembly, and I lost!

Why did I run all these races for public office?

And why did I campaign, day-in and day-out, walking to thousands of houses door-to-door, and standing in shopping centers handing our campaign literature; getting up when it was dark so I could get to factory gates before the workers came to work; giving speeches at night and going to candidate forums?

Why did I do this? Because I had a dream, and I wanted that dream so badly. You see, if you have a dream, you will work and sacrifice to get it, But it's all up to you, no one else.

Well, I didn't reach those dream of mine. But do you know something? I never thought I was a loser, and I was a failure.

And do you know why I failed so much? Because I tried so much! If you don't want to fail, then don't try because people who try will have their share of failures. You just don't give up.

I read one time that Thomas Edison tried 1,000 different filaments to use in his light bulb before he succeeded. Edison did not think he had failed all those times. He said he now knew a thousand things that didn't work.

I can't promise you great success in life. Hard work and sacrifice didn't pay off for me in my campaigns, at least not on the way I hoped. But it paid off in other ways. I was happy doing what I was doing.

However, there is one thing I can guarantee:

- you won't succeed by sitting in front of a TV all day;
- or walking around shopping malls all day;
- or sitting in a drug house!

If you want success, sit in a library, sit in a classroom, or work at a job. And that is up to you!

To be a success, you need a dream.

- Martin Luther King had a dream
- I had a dream
- Bill Clinton had his dream to be President of the United States.
- And sometimes we give up old dreams for new dreams—like
- Michael Jordan who now dreams of playing major league baseball and is happy pursuing his new dream.

You need to have your new dreams too! But not just any dream will do. Don't dream about having millions of dollars, or fancy cars, or jewelry. Those dreams will not make you a better person.

Dream about being something, or accomplishing something...not about having something.

- Dream about becoming a doctor or nurse.
- Dream about becoming a pilot or a teacher.
- Dream about being an artist or owning your own business.
- Dream about qualifying for the Olympics.
- Dream about finding a cure for the disease that kill so many.
- Dream about going to MATC or Marquette University.
- Dream about ending hatred in this world.
- Dream about being a librarian or a zookeeper.
- Dream about being a carpenter or a chef.
- Dream about being a photographer or a poet.

Remember, without a dream, you will not be any of these!
It's all up to you. Did you hear what I said? It's all up to you.

- It's up to you to take charge of your life.
- It's up to you to get an education and to continue learning throughout your life.
- It's up to you to inform yourself about your government.
- It's up to you to vote.
- It's up to you to be the best parent you can be to your children.
- It's up to you to protect the environment, to keep your yard clean, and to keep the streets and alleys in your neighborhood clean.
- It's up to you to ask for forgiveness when you have done wrong, and it's up to you to forgive someone who wrongs you.
- It's up to you to stand against injustice.
- And as we near the anniversary of the Normandy invasion on June 6, it sometimes is up to you to stop the enemy in battle.
- And sometimes it is up to you to die so that others might live and be free.

- It's up to you to do the right thing.

Let me tell you, doing the right thing isn't always easy.
You may lose friends; you may lose popularity; you may lose a job.
You may even lose your life, as did Marin Luther King Jr.
But you won't lose your self-respect or your pride, and you won't lose your soul.

Trust me! You only lose respect for yourself when you do the wrong thing.
What will it be—right or wrong? That is up to you.

Finally, remember, Martin Luther King didn't back away from doing the right thing, and he didn't quit because of obstacles.

Martin Luther King didn't say, "I can't do it." He didn't say, "We as a people can't succeed." Do you know what he said?

We shall overcome. We shall overcome the obstacles that stand between us and our dream.

And you shall overcome too. Say it to yourself when you are feeling low. Say it to yourself when the future looks dark. Say it to yourself when you feel like giving up.

Say: I shall overcome. I shall overcome someday.

It's all up to you.

LETTER – PART I
A REPLACEMENT FOR COLUMNIST ANN LANDERS

March 10, 1987

Matthew Storin:
Editorial Department
Chicago Sun-Times
401 North Wabash
Chicago, IL 60611

Dear Mr. Storin:

I have read that the Chicago Sun-Times is looking for a replacement for Ann Landers.

Look no further.

This sounds presumptuous I know, but I can provide sagacious advice, and I can do it with humor or empathy as may be appropriate. In my present job, I constantly give advice on an endless list of problems and topics. I am a teacher of emotionally disturbed high school students (since 1980) and am a member of the Wisconsin Association for Children with Behavior Disorders. If I replace Ann Landers, the big difference will be that my advice to students, parents, and other teachers will appear in print where others with similar problems can read and use it.

Before teaching ED students, I taught high school English for 13 years, and prior to that, I was a caseworker for the Waukesha County Welfare Department. From May 1974 to August 1979, I was Executive Director of the Bingo Control Board, an agency of the State of Wisconsin that regulated bingo gambling.

I do not know if you can imagine how strictly Wisconsin wrote its legislation for the regulation of the first legal gambling to be allowed in this State, but it called for creative problem-solving to satisfy the various factions who were concerned with the success of this social experiment.

Surprisingly, I found myself advising citizens on matters not limited to bingo regulation, who did not know where else to turn for answers to their problems in dealing with other state or local government agencies, the public, and even the members within the organization.

To give you an idea of how well I was received by the people whom I served, I a am submitting as testimony excerpts from letters that were sent to me. The letter show what these people thought of my advice, and they indicate the kind of response the Sun-Times can expect if I become "Bob Landers".
I ask for the opportunity to compete for the job, and I will "skip school" to pencil with me and an eraser—case I make mistakes.

Sincerely,
Robert Hoskins

LETTER – PART II
DEBUT COLUMN: REPLACING ANN LANDERS

AN OPEN LETTER TO SUN-TIMES READERS March 10, 1987

This morning I tried on an old pair of Ann Landers shoes that have been lying around a storeroom at the Sun-Times. Even though I wear a size 11 D shoe myself, I had lots of room to wiggle my toes and they felt loose in the heels.

This is my way of acknowledging I have some big shoes to fill as I begin a new column of advice to tens of thousands of readers. The shoes I fill will be old ones, but my style will be mine and so will the advice.

Let me tell you something about myself. I know the pain that life can bring, but I can testify also to the joy for those who are disheartened. My life started in Milwaukee, Wisconsin. At age eight, my father died of Hodgkins Disease. I was the oldest of four children.

Then came a stepfather and a new life on a farm 50 miles west. The life was hard, but I grew to love it and my stepfather, though love took time. The year I started high school, my mother faced death herself and was hospitalized mote than two years.

After high school, I graduated from Carroll College, married the girl next door, worked as a welfare caseworker, and then became a teacher. Along the way, I acquired more education, bills, and six children.

My wife and I were lucky parents. None of our children were ever arrested, and they all graduated from high school. This is more to the credit of their teachers in the Kettle Moraine School District than to anything I did. The only thing I take credit for is that all six passed their driver's tests on the first try.

My wife and I have been married going on 33 years. During that time, we have known hard times, sickness, bills, and deaths. We have known the heartaches of parents and the disagreements of married life. As poet Langston Hughes wrote: "Life... ain't been no crystal stair."

I love movies, spy novels, NBC Thursday night TV, sheepshead, chess, tennis, volleyball, the Green Bay Packers, music (classical, jazz, older rock), Summerfest, and the Wisconsin State. Fair. I write poetry.

I do not know if ever I can fill the shoes Ann Landers leaves behind at the Sun-Times. For now, I will try to get by stuffing paper in them with the hope I can grow into them. But I have a secret for you readers that Ann Landers does not want revealed—that woman sure has big feet!

See you tomorrow.
Robert Hoskins

LETTER
LET'S FIRE BO BLACK

July 15, 2000

To the Journal Sentinel:

Let's fire Bo Black! It is time somebody holds her accountable for the vulgarity that too often passes for entertainment at Summerfest. What a mockery of family entertainment Summerfest has become. A parent does not dare bring young children and teens to such an event.

Clearly, bands such as Blink-182 should not be allowed on stage to make fun of each other's genitalia, talk about their favorite pastime: masturbation, or have a transvestite chase around the stage with a six-foot inflatable sex organ. Nor should we tolerate the band Fenix TX whose guitarist wished: "I hope you all drive drunk and kill a family of four.

Bo Black should hire bands and comedians who can entertain without resorting to four-letter words and bathroom topics. If entertainers want to work at a great summer event, in a great city, and be paid obscene amounts of money, then Bo should make them comply with rules for decent behavior—make it part of their contract.

The Summerfest Board and the City of Milwaukee are not obligated to hire lewd and licentious acts for its summer entertainment. If Bo Black wants to hire such acts, then let them perform in her living room, not on our lakefront. It is time Ms. Black, or someone on her staff, be responsible for seeing the acts before she hires them. That way Summerfest management will not be totally ignorant when they hire bands like Blink-182 and Fenix TX.

If Bo Black will not lay down the law against gross pandering at Summerfest, then Milwaukee's leaders should hire someone who will. We need to look no further than the State Fair Director and Board do not tolerate the type of acts for which Summerfest has become notorious.

Lastly, why is Bo Black paid $187,000 a year basically to run an 11-day music festival when the Milwaukee Police Chief is paid $116,000; the Mayor $120,000; the Superintendent of Schools $147,000; and the Governor $115,000? Who is doing the important work in the community? Is it Bo Black?

Yours truly,
Robert Hoskins

LETTER
DON'T BLAME THE POLICE

April 23, 1994

To the Journal/Sentinel

Let me preface my words by saying that I have the greatest sympathy for the mother and other family members of Bruce and John Garrett who were killed when a car full of thugs crashed into them. These thugs were trying to escape from the police in a stolen car.

Sadly, Betty Jo Garrett, their mother, blames the police because they were in pursuit of the stolen car. I excuse her remarks spoken in grief. But to blame the police because they were chasing the criminal bastards is irrational, it is irresponsible, and it is wrong.

Lest others, less grieving, agree with the mother, I say that we cannot continue to blame the police when the actions of criminals and criminal suspects cause tragedy. It is the job of our police to apprehend criminals and to get them off the streets so that the public is protected from further criminal acts.

Make no mistakes, the persons fleeing the police in this case need to be off the street. Two are suspects in a murder committed Wednesday—a gun was recovered from the stolen car matching the gun in the murder. At least two are believed to be the robbers pointed a gun at an elementary school teacher when they stole her car Tuesday—the same car that killed Mrs. Garrett's two sons Friday.

Mrs.. Garrett in her grief may blame the police for the death of her sons. The rest of us must blame the persons driving the stolen car. We must put responsibility on them. We must direct our anger at them. We must condemn them. May these killers rot behind bars for causing the deaths of John and Bruce Garrett.

Robert Hoskins

LETTER
BAN HENRY AARON FROM BASEBALL

June 30, 2014

Journal Sentinel Editor:

Henry Aaron's recent visit to Milwaukee to sell his autographs (for hundreds of dollars a signature) reminded me of his racist comments about Republicans.

Like most everyone in Milwaukee, I was a fan, even after the Milwaukee Braves moved to Atlanta. When Aaron finished his career with the Milwaukee Brewers, I took two sons to see him play again at County Stadium.

But now, Hank Aaron compares me to the Klu Klux Klan because I am Republican! After I walked in a parade on Wisconsin Avenue in Milwaukee to honor Martin Luther King Jr.'s life, Aaron slanders me as a racist.

Aaron has insulted millions of Americans who vote Republican, telling us we are racist. Does Aaron not know why? It was the republicans who passed the post-Civil War constitutional amendments ending slavery and granting citizenship to African-Americans. It was the Republicans in Congress who provided the votes for the Civil Rights Act and the Voting Rights Act in the 1960's.

But today, Aaron insults half of the voters in America comparing

Republicans to the KKK because we do not agree with President Obama. For this, Baseball Commissioner Bud Selig should ban Aaron from baseball if he does not apologize for his racist remarks.

Selig needs to act as swiftly as Basketball Commissioner Adam Silver acted in banning Donald Sterling, owner of the Los Angeles Clippers. At least Sterling did not speak his racist remarks publicly and has apologized. Selig banned Pete Rose from baseball for betting on baseball games, but Aaron's racism is worse than Rose betting on games since Aaron's remarks speak to the heart of America and who we are as a people.

Speaking for myself, should Hank Aaron apologize, I will accept his apology on behalf of my great-grandfather, Jacob Hoskins, who served at Gettysburg, at Petersburg under General Ulysses Grant, and at other places in between during the Civil War.

Robert Hoskins

LETTER
DEDICATED AND DECENT?

May 8, 1997

To the Journal Sentinel Editor:

I wish to reply to the letter of Hy Pitts in the Journal Sentinel in which he/she decried efforts to recall Senators Herb Kohl and Russ Feingold. Pitts described our senators as "dedicated" and "decent".

Dedicated and decent? When they vote to kill babies that are partially born by snipping off their heads or suctioning their brain matter? Not by my definition are Kohl and Feingold decent or dedicated.

Then, Pitts labeled opponents of Kohl and Feingold as "single-minded, one-dimensional fanatics" who insult the democratic process. The opponents of partial birth abortion are no more single-minded than the abolitionists who fought slavery in the 1800's, or the Germans and others who opposed the Nazis treatment of Jews. These people were also single-minded.

And please explain how citizens using the tools of democracy (petition and recall) are insulting the democratic process? Whether Pitts knows it or not, petition and recall are part of the democratic process!

When a single issue like partial birth abortion is so momentous that it draws the line between being civilized and being barbaric, or it goes to the heart of being human or beast, then other issues pale into insignificance.

It is true that neither Kohl nor Feingold has voted to maintain slavery or to put people into concentration camps. They just vote to kill babies that are still partially in their mothers' womb.

To me that is deserving of recall.

Sincerely,
Robert Hoskins

LETTER
A VERY MINOR CRIME

February 12, 2001

District Attorney
Brian Blanchard
Dane County Court House
Madison, Wisconsin

Dear Attorney Blanchard,

Let me assume that you probably are not fully informed about all the cases currently being prosecuted by your office. However, since you are the new district attorney, I am writing to ask why your office insists on trying the case against Tim Jennings a second time. A jury earlier in November, 2000 split 6-6 on the prosecutor's case.

It would seem to me that your office would have more important work than to pursue the case against Mr. Jennings. The charge against him did not even warrant the first trial. The case was so insignificant that even if the charge were true (which he denies), the case is a waste of public resources.

A little history. Mr. Jennings was charged with violating a court restraining order that he stay away from a woman he knew from church and from a Sentry Food Store where they had worked together and where he also shopped. His offensive behavior was that he had taken pictures of the woman on public street where I think any citizen has the right to aim a camera.

But, the court accepted the woman's word that Mr. Jennings was harassing her and issued an order that he stay away from her. How far? 10 feet? 50 feet? 100 feet? A mile? Mr. Jennings claims that the order did not specify.

Mr. Jennings, in fear of going to jail, obeyed the order in good faith. He never spoke to the woman, he never telephoned her, he never went by her home or workplace, never wrote to her, never took her picture.

So what happened? Mr. Jennings goes to Holy Redeemer Church for Mass on a Saturday night as was his weekly practice. As usual, he is there early and sits in the front of the church. When the Mass begins,the priest and servers walk up the center aisle from the back of the church. Tim rises, as do nearly all attendants at the service, and turns to watch the procession.

At the very back of the church, more than 50 feet as stated in the trial, the woman stands with a friend. They apparently leave and report Tim to the police charging that Tim gave them "the finger" as the priest and others in the procession started down the aisle. Apparently, nobody else, including the priest and nearby parishioners, witnessed this action. Tim's defense is that they may have seen him making the sign of the cross which he always does.

Nevertheless, Tim is arrested in the church, escorted to a police vehicle on nearby State Street, and taken to jail where he was confined until the following Monday afternoon. This happened on the word of the woman in back of the church, which was hardly well-lit for evening service.

Whether Mr. Jennings did, or did not do, as the woman reported to police, a jury split evenly on the charge that he violated the court's order. Now, the question is: does the charge merit a second jury trial using the court's and public defender's time? It is often complained that the courts are too crowded. Is not the charge in Mr. Jennings' case a minor infraction of the law? Should the resources of Dane County be squandered on a second trial?

Furthermore, what happens if the prosecution wins? Does your office intend to put Mr. Jennings in jail for giving someone the finger assuming that he did? Is that what the office wants: jail time for this? Or does it want probation in a system that has trouble monitoring serious offenders because the system is overburdened?

The irony is that the court restraining order, allegedly violated in October 1999, expired in July 2000. If Mr. Jennings had wanted, He could have resumed picture-taking again. But, he hasn't. He had no contact with the woman while under the restraining order, and he has not had contact with her in the seven months since the order has expired. Just what is the purpose of another trial, and if the prosecution loses a second time, will there be a third and fourth trial?

Please use your discretion and end this matter. Mr. Jennings already spent two days in jail on the charge, guilty or not. Does the matter deserve more?

Sincerely,

Robert Hoskins

LETTER
KEEP OPEN THE WAUKESHA COUNTY HOME

April 2, 1986

TO THE EDITOR:

According to State Senator J.M. Davis, Waukesha County "should get out of the nursing home business."He has criticized county officials for not looking seriously at turning the operation of Northview Nursing Home over to the private sector.

Why should the county get out of the nursing home business? The care of the elderly and chronically ill is a proper role of government. That is one of the basic reasons for government to exists: to care for the needy and those no one else will care for.

Waukesha County and state officials need to get their priorities straight. The care of the ill and elderly on any scale ranks ahead of the county operating golf courses and boat launchings; it ranks ahead of running an airport for a few citizens who fly airplanes; it ranks ahead of operating a county fair, a museum, or an exposition building used for horse shows and concerts. Where is the cry to place these operations in the private sector?

We should question county officials about the difference between operating an airport and a nursing home. Some county board members want an expanded airport with longer runways. The cost is reported at $5.3 million. In fact, the county recently paid $1,000,000 for a farm to acquire a land for the airport. Waukesha County has sought more than $8,000,000 in aid for the airport in 1986, and it received $1,175,400 since 1984, mostly for lights and smaller construction projects such as taxiways and hanger aprons. I do not hear any outcry from Senator Davis or county officials to turn the airport over the to the private sector.

In the last analysis, what do the advocates of closing the Northview Home claim as a benefit? They claim lower cost if the home is run privately. But, as everybody knows, the lower cost will be achieved by lower wages paid to the people who will be doing the caring. Will the cost of heating the building be less if Northview is run privately? Will the cost of electricity and utilities be less? Will the cost for food for the patients be less? Where will the savings come from?

The saving will be at the expense of the home and nursing staff who clean the blood, the vomit, and the human feces off the elderly, and dress and feed them. I am not advocating salary cuts for county employees, but if cuts are needed in the county's budget, then they should start in the courthouse, not at Northview. It is a lot harder and dirtier work to lift patients and clean their bodies and laundry than to file documents, collect fees, type letters, or do any of the other jobs performed in the courthouse.

All jobs in county government are probably necessary, and I do not mean to lessen the importance of the people in those positions. But the people who work at Northview, as well as other nursing homes, are unsung heroes. They deserve to be paid according to the importance of their jobs, and whose job is more important caring for human beings, most of whom are ill, dying, and lonely. It is not a job I would want to do.

So, any elected officials who tell me that running Northview privately will save me money as a taxpayer deserves to be challenged. They lack any kind of courage to go to the Northview staff and tell them that they are overpaid for what they do. They are afraid to cut the salaries of the staff themselves and are content to let others do their dirty work. That is not a reason for the county to get out of the nursing home business.

County and state officials need to get their priorities straight. Caring for the needy is one of the most basic reasons for government to exist. That is among the reasons why we pay taxes: so that those in need are cared for. Before the county gets out of the nursing home business, elected officials should look at a few other business to divest first.

Robert Hoskins
Delafield, WI

LETTER
SHOULD I BE FIRED?

March 18, 2007

Tina Dayne, Director
Human Resources
West Allis School District
West Allis, WI 53227

Dear Director Dayne:

Since our meeting March 15, 2007, I have done a great deal of thinking about the accusation that I do not follow teacher lesson plans.

As I informed you, this is not true. At the start of every class, I read the teacher's instructions to the class and write them on the board. For the history classes in question, the plans called for students to be given a test. As I remember, they were allowed 20 minutes. I distributed the tests and wrote both the starting and ending times on the chalk board. When time expired. I collected the tests. The remaining class time was to be used by students to work on their "fireside speeches"project which I allowed the students to do. However, because of a shortened class schedule, students did not have much time as usually afforded by a full class period.

The sociology or psychology class was to be shown a video the whole period, which I showed except for the time when I took the class to the auditorium for the assembly program. For these reasons, I request that the teacher explain how I failed to follow her plans, and I would like to be able to respond to any specifics.

Furthermore, I did not criticize the teacher's test or the teacher. I never criticize a teacher, nor do I allow students remarks about a teacher to go unchallenged. If a student describes a problem or expresses criticism of a teacher, I tell them to discuss it with their teacher. If the student responds that the teacher will not do anything, then I tell them to talk to their principal or guidance counselor.

Regarding my alleged criticism of the test, I did not criticize, I explained one or two questions. A particular question as I remember was true-false: The U.S. policy was not to "attack" Japan, but attack Germany first. (I do not remember the exact wording, but the word "attack" was used.)

I simply told students that if they get the answers wrong, they should discuss their answer with the teacher because the answer can be debated. I reminded them that in the movie "Pearl Harbor", the famous air raid on Japanese cities was as "attack" on Japan launched from air craft carriers, and I mentioned the US. "attack"on the Japanese fleet at Midway soon after Pearl Harbor. This was an explanation that the answer could be debated, not a criticism of the test, and I said this after the test was over.

I also told the classes that I had heard on the radio that morning that this day marked the end of the battle for Guadalcanal, a battle that had waged from August 1942 to February 1943. I do not think my calling attention to the Guadalcanal victory should be interpreted as criticism of the teacher or of the test.

In conclusion, the only way I can be guilty of NOT following the lesson plan would have been if I had not given the test to the classes; or if I had told the students to work on a different project; or in sociology, if I had shown a different video to the class than the one provided! Certainly, I did not do any of these things.

Finally, I acknowledge that the teacher has every right to request that I not be assigned to her classes if she does not want me, whatever the reason.

However, I do not see how her personal complaint should bar me from assignment in other teachers' classes, especially if they have voiced no complaints themselves.

I am a good teacher. I have been a substitute teacher at West Allis for 15 years. I do what I am expected to do. Prior to substituting, I taught for 27 years, including ED and LD classes. I have a master's degree as well as all the credits for second master's degree in Exceptional Education for which I am certified and licensed. I have over 200 college and university credits, and I scored in the 99th percentile on the Graduate Record Exam in Education— the highest ever scored at Carroll College and possibly the highest: in the nation.

I anticipate your reply.

Sincerely
Robert Hoskins

LETTER
AN HONORABLE LAWYER

Allen E. Schwartz
Attorney At Law
603 W. Main Avenue
Knoxville, TN 37902

Dear Allen:

I want to tell you how grateful I am to you for helping me receive justice. I was in the right in my case, but I know that being in the right too often is not enough to win in the courts.

Living in Wisconsin, I needed an attorney in Knoxville, Tennessee, where I knew not a soul. Moreover, my case was small and there was no prospect of a lucrative settlement for a lawyer willing to represent me. But you took my case, for which I will be forever indebted to you.

My case was repayment of money owed to me; but for me, it was more about principle and the ethics of Richard McConnell, a member of the legal profession and a federal administrative law judge in Knoxville.

You stood fearless, and at some risk to yourself in taking my case, for I know that somewhere down the road, McConnell may be in a position to hurt you in a case. Most lawyers would not have bothered with my case since it was not worth their time. You took the case and pursued it to victory!

The fact that you took my case is evidence to me that you care about justice, principle, and the ethics of public persons. The community of Knoxville is better in having you as a member.

Please feel free to call upon me if I can ever be of help to you, whatever the matter may concern.

Yours truly,

Robert Hoskins

LETTER
TILTING THE EXPERIENCE METRIC

September 8, 2008

To the Journal Sentinel Editor:
I challenge the fairness of the Journal Sentinel editorial, dated September 5th, which questioned whether John McCain, Republican candidate for President, can deliver on his "worthy goals". I have not read that the editors have asked whether Democratic candidate Barack Obama can deliver on anything he has promised.

Also, the editors said, "Sarah Palin [McCain's selection for VP] fails on the experience metric. . ." but where has the Journal Sentinel pointed out that Obama fails on the "experience metric"himself by having even less experience than Palin—and he is running for President!

And while the editor implies McCain may not be "the most effective change agent. What change did he effect when he voted "Present" 135 times as an Illinois state senator? How has Obama been an agent of change when he has not introduced any legislation of consequence as a U.S. Senator?

The Journal Sentinel should know: Actions are what speak louder than words.

Sincerely,

Robert Hoskins

LETTER
SMELLY SOCKS

February 22, 2019

Milwaukee Journal Sentinel
LETTER TO THE EDITOR

My, My!

The City of Milwaukee is honoring ex-football player, Colin Kaeperncik, during Black History Month. How wonderful and deserving is this choice by our city's fathers.

After our city recently ended a week of honoring slain police officer Matthew Rittner, who was shot to death in the line of duty, we now turn to honoring an ex-football player who refuses to stand for national anthem, but more damnable, wore socks reading that the police are PIGS!

What hypocrites we have leading the City of Milwaukee that we should honor such an individual. What shame they bring to the people of Milwaukee!
In view of their shameful choice wrought by these city leaders, I suggest they present Kaepernick with a different pair of socks as an award -- since the pair he wears stinks a foul odor.

Sincerely,

Robert (Rob) Hoskins

LETTER
SCARED OF WHAT?

Milwaukee Journal Sentinel

To the Editor:

Oh how ridiculous are the comments of some Milwaukee residents regarding the upcoming Republican National Convention. The Journal Sentinel headline, on the front page of its June 24, 2024 edition, blared the remark of Angela Lang, executive of BLOC (Black Leaders Organizing for Communities) "I'm actually scared".

Scared? Scared of what?

She's scared of former President Donald Trump's arrival in Milwaukee for the Republican Convention. According to the article, she is worried that it could turn the event "into a powder keg".

Lang fears that Trump's sentencing in New York "could embolden... RNC attendees who are more radicalized against communities of color, especially in Milwaukee."

What? She fears the Republican delegates and visitors coming to our city? It isn't the Milwaukee residents who should be scared! It is the Republican visitors who should be shaking in their boots.

It wasn't Republicans who shot 13 people Wednesday, as reported in the Journal Sentinel newspaper today (June 28, 2024). And certainly, Republicans did not shoot any of the other 273 nonfatal victims shot this year, or any of the 837 victims shot last year, not including 172 homicides.

So my hope is that attendees and visitors to the Republican Convention enjoy themselves while in Milwaukee and that return home safely after Convention is over.

And I further hope is that attendees and visitors to the Republican leave, residents like Angela Lang can relax and feel safe again in their homes and in the streets of our fair city.

Robert Hoskins

telp. 414 248-6513

LETTER
A HERO WHO HAS DIED

To the Editor:

Today is May 23, 2024, and I read in the newspaper that today a hero will be buried at a cemetery in Waukesha, Wisconsin.

Her name is Jadwiga Przydryga.

She will be buried in America though she was born in Poland, and though I did not know her, I wish I had.

I read in her obituary: "At age 16, Jadwiga enlisted to join the Polish underground resistance. "She and her childhood friends (along with others) defended the streets of Warsaw, resisting the Nazi occupation.

In August 1944, when the Warsaw Uprising began, she and thousands of Poles fought the German Army in the streets of Warsaw for two months. Outnumbered and needing arms and ammunition, they lost -- 250,000 poles had died.

Jadwiga was arrested as were other survivors of the uprising, and she became a prisoner of war at age 17. She was confined at the Oberlangen camp in Germany until 12, 1945, when Polish troops of the 1st Polish Armoured Division liberated the camp.

Following the end of the war, Jadwiga journeyed to London, England to rejoin the Polish Home Army which was operating under the Polish government in exile. In London, her obituary says: she met her future husband, Zbigniew Przydryga, himself a partisan fighter and fellow survivor.

They immigrated to America and pursued the American Dream where they built a beautiful home and "filled it with love, laughter, food, music and dancing."

Good for them!

Jadwiga, I salute you on your way to Heaven after a lifr well-lived with valor. Your family is entitled to be proud.

Rest in Peace.

From Robert Hoskins

EULOGY FOR MIKE DEJANOVICH

I am not here to tell you that Mike was saint. He wasn't. But he had a big heart; he was generous. He would give you the shirt off his back.

And he was better to my mother than I am. She was in many ways his mother, and he treated her as such after his own mother had died.

Many a Sunday morning after church, Mike would be over to my mother and Bert's house, and he would make breakfast or bring something like bakery – or mow the lawn or clear the driveway of snow.

As well as the family he was born into, he was also a part of my family as anyone can tell by the nieces and nephews that are here to say goodbye to Uncle Mike. He will forever remain a member of the family.

I should say that Mike too often took risks. In playing sheepshead (that's a card game for the uninitiated), Mike would often pick the blinds on a "nothing hand." Sometimes, he would win, but just as often he would lose. Still, he would take the risk.

And Mike had dreams.
He always planned to retire in his 50's and live off investments and pension.

Some dreams don't come true.

One of my lasting memories that I will take to my grave is Father's Day about 1980—my brother Larry was to die in a few months, unbeknown st to any of us at the time.

The memory is the five brothers-in-law: Mike, Larry, Dick Lampe, Tom Niese, and I went to Dick's cabin at Bid Flats. We drank beer, played cards, went fishing, and hiked through the woods. At least, it was woods before Dick had caused a forest fire the year before. We climbed over burnt trees still charred and black.

It was a good time, the five brothers together. But that was when Larry had learned that he had cancer. Now, Mike is dead too. Dick was lucky, however. He had open-heart surgery before his heart had damage.

All of us who knew Larry miss him. Now, all of us who knew Mike will miss him just as much.

For Sue, who was married to Mike this past year, their life together was short, but I hope it was sweet. Now, it is over soon.

Over the years, I told a number of people that Mike reminded me of the movie star Robert Mitchum. He looked like Mitchum to me. And I remember how strong Mike was. I saw him ring the bell three times, swinging the hammer with one hand at one of those carnival games.

Mike was decent man. I will miss his hearty laugh, his reckless card playing at times. Now, if I want to see him, I have to go to a video store and rent a Robert Mitchum movie.

EULOGY FOR ISABELLE MUNDSCHAU

I hope so many of us today, do not remember my mother as an old, forgetful, and sometimes too stubborn a woman:

A woman who would wash a few more dishes, or feed the birds in her yard, or water some plants when we were trying to drag her out the door when she had to go somewhere;

A woman who would not leave bread at restaurant when she could feed it to her birds, and who took unused pads of butter, packets of sugar, and coffee cream because they were on our table.

She was too stubborn.

And she would not give up her mission to tell the story of her vision of the Blessed Mother.

Many times, my sisters, Bert, or I would be frustrated when she insisted on telling her story to strangers.

It was even more frustrating when we tried to stop her from repeating her story to people who had heard it before, but were nevertheless, polite enough to listen again.

But my mother wasn't always the old woman who lies in this coffin. She wasn't old all her life. She wasn't always forgetful. Once, she was young. And her stubbornness, when she was young, was a strength, not a fault.

Just last week, seven days ago, we buried Uncle Gordy, my mother's brother. And at his funeral, I spoke of Uncle Gordy's courage; how he embraced life in the face of pain, disability, and hardship.

Well, strength, courage, and faith run in the family.
My mother was the same as her brother, and I never heard her complain about the crosses she had to bear. She was too stubborn to put down the crosses in life, no matter how heavy the weight.

Let me tell you about my mother's life.

Her mother-in-law, who lived with us, died in our home in 1940.

Her own mother died in 1941. Her father died in 1942.

And her husband, who had Hodgkins' Disease during this time, died January 12, 1944. In four years, she lost them all, and she left with our four children to raise, and with two younger brothers who were orphans.

She was barely 29 years old.

I am glad that my mother was stubborn.
I am glad that she did not let grief rule her.
I am glad that she did not let depression and self-pity conquer her spirit.

She was strong.

Then, at age 35, she fought death.
She survived two years in a hospital bed at the Jefferson Co. Sanitorium: She could not see her children except from an upper floor window. You think Death did not come to get my mother when she was ill?

Let me tell you of her dream.

When my mother had married, she had a friend who could not attend the wedding because she was dying. Instead, my mother and the wedding party went to see her. After that day, my mother never saw her friend again. The friend died.

Fifteen years later, as my mother lay bedridden, the friend came to her in a dream. She said: "Isabelle, come with me. We have to catch the train. It leaves at 3:10."

My mother told her: "I can't come with you.
I have to stay with my children. They need me."

The friend insisted that my mother come with her. But my mother refused. At that point, my mother woke. For awhile, she lay in bed, in the darkness. Then she pressed the call button for the nurse to request a bed pan.
As the nurse attended to her, my mother asked what time it was. The nurse said 3:10, and as she spoke, a train whistle sounded as a train went through Jefferson.

My mother did not take the train that night.
Instead, she stayed behind for her children.
Only a dream! A friend from the dead coming for her?

Yes! My mother was a strong woman.

She climbed mountains some of us will never climb; suffered loses some of us will never suffer; and she had a faith in God stronger than many of us will ever know.

May God grant each of you the strength to carry your own crosses in life as my mother did in hers.

ROBERT HOSKINS
March 25, 2003

EULOGY FOR GORDON JOHANN

"Cowards die many times before their deaths;
The valiant never taste of death but once.
Of all the wonders that I yet have heard,
It seems to me most strange that men should fear,
Seeing that death, a necessary end,
Will come when it will come".
Julius Caesar

2,044 years ago, almost to this day, was the funeral of Julius Caesar. But unlike Marc Antony, I do not come to bury Uncle Gordy; I come to praise him.

Gordy was no coward. He was brave. For so many years, he faced pain and disability with courage, not complaint. Never, ever, did I hear him say, "Why me?" Why me God?" Instead, he took crutches and later hid wheelchair, and went about living life.

Eventually, Gordy would virtually lose the use of fingers—he could hardly hold a spoon, or turn the page of a newspaper or book, or hold a
 letter.

How, would I face such days? How would you? But we all know how Uncle Gordy faced them. We were witnesses.

When he was with us, he laughed, played cards, drank a little beer, and suffered any pain in silence. His was a quiet bravery.

Gordy did not hide from life, he embraced it. He did not isolate himself, but dwelt among us. He lived, he traveled, he joined us at all the family events, he visited us in our homes. He lived life.

How many times did I hear him say, "Oh, don't worry about me. Take care of yourself."

As the years of Uncle Gordy's life wound down, he loved to reminisce about the days when he and I rode the milk routes for my dad, Gib Wendt.

He remembered the names of the shippers, of other milk haulers who hauled for Hoard's Creamery and Hawthorne-Melody, even remembering what trucks they drove.

We would stop at the Eat-Mor Restaurant where we served by Pappy, Rollie, and Roger; and I would remind Gordy how he made one of the bigger mistakes of hid life—he was going to fill me up with hamburgers and chocolate malts.

That's what he thought, but I was in my prime. After two malts and two or three hamburgerd, I could still have eaten more.

Later in life, when I was an adult, I was to win a hot dog eating contest at the State Fair. But the Eat-Mor was where I trained as a youth, and Uncle Gordy was my sponsor.

The sad thing for me is that now I have no one with whom I can reminisce about our days in the milk hauling business, or lunches at the Eat-Mor, or the radio shows we listened to. Those days are gone. They passed with Uncle Gordy.

In the end, Uncle Gordy did not fear death. Several times over the last couple years, he told me that he was ready to go, that he had lived a good life. Those were hid words: "I'm ready to go; I've lived a good life."

Gordy knew that death was a necessary end, and it will come when it will come.

While Gordy was not the noblest Roman of them all—Shakespeare had used that description for Brutus—Gordy was noble, and he lived life as a noble should live it—with family, and country and faith foremost in importance.

Uncle Gordy was my mother's brother.
He was my driver on the milk routes,
and for my children and grandchildren,
for my brothers and sisters, and for their children, he was OUR UNCLE GORDY.

Rest in peace!

ROBERT HOSKINS
March 18, 2003

EULOGY FOR
NANCY HOSKINS NIESE

God choices the strong from among us to serve as heroic models to the rest of mankind.

God saw my sister Nancy and my brother-in-law Tom as two people having the qualities that the rest of us need to witness: strength and faith, family and love, devotion and sacrifice.

So, Nancy got cancer, and we all witnessed her suffering—especially the final days.

But we also witnessed the family's heroics. Her husband Tom—devoted, steadfast, until death do they part. Her children: Natalie, Valerie, and Bryan who attended, cared, and encouraged her until death came.

I know Tom asked, "Why God?"
I know that his faith in God was challenged as he prayed and watched Nancy suffer, and I know he feels anger toward God for the terrible ordeal that has been wrought upon their family.

And why shouldn't he feel anger? Granted, we are faithful servants of God, but we were created with free will. We will not go quietly into the night. We want answers from God and accountability for our human suffering.

Still, day after day, after day, we watched Nancy suffer. Now we are drained of our tears; now we are exhausted after weeks and months of watching her life reach its end. And we are sad that our prayers seem to have gone unanswered.

But lest we be sad too long, and lest we carry anger too far, and lest we lose faith in God and hope for salvation, let me tell you some "good news."

We witnessed a miracle.

Doubt me if you want, but I believe a miracle occurred. I know what I witnessed. Sometimes, we are too close to a situation to realize when prayers are answered.

Let me tell you about it.

At the time our mother died in March 2003, I did not know who would die first, Nancy or our mother. Nancy could not keep down food, she was being sustained with tubes, she weighted less than 100 pounds. She needed an operation.

Many people were praying for Nancy. I was praying to Saint Peregrine, the patron saint of cancer victims. When Mary Ann bought a small statue of St. Peregrine at St. Josaphat Basilica, I suggested that we ask Father Robert Joseph to bless it for Nancy.

Father told us that he had been to Italy, to the hometown or shine of St. Peregrine, and that he had bought back oil to anoint the sick. He offered to bless and anoint Nancy. So, it was arranged.

I do not remember the exact chronology, but a miracle occurred, and I attribute it to St. Peregrine. Nancy went ahead with the operation. The tumor in her stomach was bypassed, and slowly, Nancy was able to keep down food. Out came the tubes, and Nancy regained her weight—35 pounds.

Think of it! An operation with a 3%-5% chance of success.
Think of it! She had only months to live, and her daughter Valerie and her

husband-to-be (also named Tom) rushed their wedding plans so that Nancy could be present when they married.

But Nancy didn't die, she lived.

She lived two more years.

Tomorrow, I will walk to Nancy's grave, knowing in my soul that God answered our prayers and gave Nancy an extension of life.

I know there were hard days that Nancy went through, but there were good days too. She witnessed Valerie's wedding; she and Tom traveled to our sister Laura's home in Texas; and last October, and we all shared a trip to Branson: my sister Kathy, our Aunt Lona, Mary Ann and me, and Tom and Nancy.

In Branson, we met our sister Laura and Ray, and all of us stayed at the same motel, and laughed ourselves silly at the Jim Stafford show and at Yakov Smirnoff's life story. We spent hours talking in the van together as we traveled. I thanked God for the memory of that last trip.

Earlier this year, Nancy and Tom enjoyed a trip to Florida, and in June, Nancy danced the jitterbug with Uncle Jerry at my granddaughter Octavia's wedding.

Nancy enjoyed the extra time God gave her, especially the extra time to do things with her daughters, Nathalie and Valerie, with her son Bryan, and with granddaughter Alyssa. And she welcomed the visits of dear friends and family. She used the time wisely.

Nancy was dear us. While She was certainly afraid to die, she set a standard for us to be brave. Her smile was always evident as she recognized friends and family who entered her room. She did not lose faith.

Not only was Nancy brave, but so were Tom and the children. In the face of death by cancer, they fought to sustain Nancy's life. They tried to move mountains, and sometimes the mountain budged.

Now, all of us must go on with our lives. And to Nancy's children who loved her with such devotion: live your lives so that your mother would be proud of you, do what is right, be forgiving, strive to be saints though you are bound to stumble, raise your children with love, and honor your father for all of his days.

I'll see you in Heaven, Nancy!

EULOGY FOR
GERALD JOHANN

The voice of Donald Duck has been silenced. No more will young members of our families hear Uncle Jerry do hi imitation.

I might add that card games throughout the Milwaukee area will be quieter too.

Some of you may have noticed Jerry's T-shirt that says, "World Champion Sheepshead Team." Don't be misled! Though Jerry sometimes won a few dollars playing cards, he never qualified for the team because he did not know the rules of sheepshead well enough.

With Jerry, a little knowledge was not so much a dangerous thing, as it was an inflated thing—inflated with hot air. One time we were playing sheepshead at his house when he got into a rare disagreement. (Not with me obviously, because Jerry and I never argued.)

No! Jerry crossed words with none other than Tom Pinter. And to win his point, Jerry cited a rule int the Book of Hoyle as his authority.

Tom countered that there was no such rule in Hoyle. To my credit, I served as a calming influence on these two loud partisans. I figured someone had to serve as a peacemaker, and I was more than qualified.

Finally, the argument led to a challenge: How much do you want to bet?

Five Dollars! Well, knowing a sure thing when I see it, I also took Jerry's bet!

So, Jerry got the famous book to prove his point. He looked, and he looked, and he looked, and he looked. Guess what? This is true. When we went home that night. Jerry had resumed his search.

And Tom and I, we are still looking for our $5.00.

As much as Jerry needed help to be a good Sheepshead player, he stood alone as a superb athlete. He was honorable mention all-state Illinois fullback as a sophomore at Mooseheart.

He was a good basketball player and an extremely accurate free throw shooter, even in his 70's.

He was a reckless volleyball player and a ping pong whiz.

He was a ringer in horseshoe and jarts.

I don't know how good a swimmer he was, but he was a fearless diver off the high dive. Also track and field.

You named it, Jerry probably excelled at it, and in his elder years, he participated in Senior Olympics very successfully. It is a wonder that all that skill never carried over to card playing.

Before Jerry died, he expressed his thanks to his card playing group and to all his camping, ping pong, horseshoe, bowling, and Senior Olympic friends. He appreciated their competition, encouragement, and sportsmanship.

Playing cards with Jerry, we all were used to hearing Jerry say in his soft-spoken voice: "Shuffle the damn cards!" (This usually happened when he was dealt a lousy hand.)

So, for Christmas, Tom Pinter bought Jerry a present: a card shuffling machine. It was a gift of love, a perfect gift, a practical gift, something Jerry could use.

Do you know what Jerry said after he opened it? "Pinter, where are the batteries? How can I use it without batteries?" Well, for weeks, even months, the machine sat unused until Tom broke down and bought Jerry some batteries.

In the months and years that have since passed, Jerry softened toward Tom, and he often referred to Tom's gift as "that piece of crap".

Jerry, my brother Larry, and I grew up together, and Jerry was more a brother than an uncle. We played together as kids rolling in the grassy yard where my grandparents lived on 27th and Vine street. And my mother would be unhappy when we got grass stains on our pants.

We played in the basement once with a BB gun, and I shot a big, round circle in a window about the size of a grapefruit.

Larry and I helped moved Lona and Jerry to their house on 23rd Street, and later I often stayed overnight at Jerry and Lona's when I was taking classes at UW-M. This I did off and on from 1967 to 1985.

During this years, Jerry and I played many games of casino at the dining room table. Regretably, I have to report that Jerry won more games than I won. But as I always said: "Jerry was lucky at cards!"

So, now the end has come for Jerry, and the end was not so bad, considering that the end was death, Jerry wished it. He did not fear it.

Now, like all of you, I will miss Jerry, I will miss him dearly. For so, so many years, he and I rode together when our sheepshead games were out in the Oconomowoc area.

This past Wednesday, I was out there for a game when I received the news that Jerry had died. That night, I drove home alone. The seat beside me in the car was empty. I missed him. A part of my life is empty.

I hope Jerry can hear my words above the welcoming trumpets and harp music playing for his arrival.

Jerry! Until more of us get there, the guys say you should keep busy in Heaven by cooling the beer, dealing the cards, and counting out the chips.

Oh, and don't forget to keep the 'bible' near the game. Make sure it's the Revised Edition of Hoyle so you can learn the rules.

We'll see you in Heaven someday. Keep the Gates open for us.

EULOGY FOR NEAL LEHNERT — February 27, 2017

WELCOME:

Last Tuesday was a sad day. It was 6 o'clock in the morning when the phone rang. When the caller said, "It's Chasity, Neal and Kathy's daughter," I knew immediately.

I said, "Your Dad died," even as she spoke the words herself. My friend of 50 years was dead.

Neal first showed up in my life as a sophomore in my freshman English class at Oconomowoc High School.

That's right—a sophomore in my freshman English class.

You see, Neal was repeating ninth grade English—he had failed the class the year before. Hard to believe, isn't it? But by the end of the year, I passed him with a 'D.'

As Neal often bragged, he never opened a textbook, but he listened in my class.

That was true. Neal listened in class and in life. He was a talker, but he listened well. How else could he disagree with you?

Some people would say that Neal liked to argue. Not me! I would say that he liked to debate. There is difference.

Debate is the purpose of enlightenment and the challenge of proving a point. And Neal was very good in debate, even for a kid who never opened a textbook.

I tell you this because so many times over the years I thought to myself: wouldn't it be great if Neal and I had been lawyers together, representing people who needed justice?

We'd have made a great team — Hoskins and Lehnert, or as Neal would have argued: Lehnert and Hoskins Law Firm.

Sometimes, I think about what should have been.

Since Neal's death, my memory has been working overtime.

I remember Neal as a student stopping at my classroom after school, and we would wad paper from the wastebasket into balls and shoot baskets. Whoever lost these contests had to buy snacks.

Afterward, we'd stop at a hole-in-the-wall food stand, next to Albert's gas station in Oconomowoc, and loser paid.

We probably split 50/50 in our competition. Neal was no Pistol Pete Marovich or Michael Jordan, but then, neither was I.

Of course, I had to give Neal a ride home afterwards because he missed the school bus.

I also remember Neal was a salesman in high school. He sold Watkin's products: mostly to teachers. I would buy a drink powder from him—like Kool Aide—as well as vanilla extract and occasionally other items.

Later, Neal owned a Watkin's store when he was married.

I remember Neal was kicked off the school bus. He and his father came to my home in Delafield one night to discuss strategy to get him back on the bus. I think Neal talked to a lawyer, Harry Rummel, for free advice as well.

What I don't remember is how Neal and Kathy showed up at my motel in Nashville, TN, to sleep in my room during the day while I attended a songwriter conference at the Vanderbilt Hotel.

When I got back that afternoon, they were gone. I must have told Neal where I would be staying; otherwise, I don't know how he would have known I was there.

One thing that I do remember is St. Patrick's Day when Neal and Kathy, Mary Ann and I went to an Irish bar on St. Paul Ave. in Milwaukee because a real Irish band from Ireland would be playing.
That night I got angry.

The Irish band wouldn't play requests for songs such as 'Danny Boy' or 'When Irish Eyes Are Smiling.' They said the songs weren't Irish – they weren't authentic.

Instead, they played songs about sailing the sea. Really? I wasn't going to listen. I let the band know I didn't like its selection songs.

I didn't want to hear songs about sailing the sea. I wanted songs about Peg (of my heart) and about Kathleen (whom I wanted to take home again).

That is when I decided that Neal was a peacemaker. He wanted me to stay calm, not get excited, not start a fight. So the four of us walked out.

We went to Katie's Diner down the street to eat corn beef and cabbage. And we saw the table where President Bill Clinton sat when he ate there on a visit to Milwaukee.

Looking back, there were occasions where I did enjoy the music—though it wasn't Irish. One was a night at Aliota's on Bluemound Road where Paul Patterson played the piano.

That night, Kathy sang songs to Paul's accompaniment, and he complimented her on her voice as did others at the bar.

The other occasion was at a bar in West Allis across from the State Fair Park. Chasity was singing with a band; she sounded good. I had hope that she would make it into the big time.

However, it was not to be, though I think it was good that Chasity chased the rainbow.

I have to mention a memory of more recent vintage. For many years, going back to the early 1970's, I was invited to Neal's and Kathy's New Year's Eve parties at their home at Grand Ave. That's when our run of welcoming the New Year together started.

Thereafter, we continued to welcome each New Year together until Neal broke his leg and was in a nursing home for months.

I'm sure Neal thought that our consecutive string would be ending. But Mary Ann and I went to see him at the nursing home that New Year's Eve, and I smuggled in a bottle of Bailey's Irish Cream.

Mary Ann and I stayed until it was time for us to leave for late movie. Before leaving, the four of us—Neal, Kathy, Mary Ann, and I—drank Bailey's to toast the New Year.

Incidentally, this year Neal told me that he didn't expect to see another New Year.

Besides each New Year and St. Patrick's Day, Neal and Kathy started celebrating the 4th of July with our families.

For most of the day, we relaxed at Legend Park in Franklin, and the day ended with everyone watching the fireworks after dark—which is not to say that fireworks were not possible during the day if discussions got too heated.

Such was our friendship that lasted to his death.

We all know that Neal was blessed with good health: diabetes, kidney dialysis, heart problems, and eventually a kidney transplant—he suffered all of these.

But to be honest, Neal talked about his problems by the way of explanation, not by way of complaint. I believe he accepted his health as God gave it to him.

Though Neal was not blessed with good health, God did bless him in another way: He gave Neal a wife of strength, and loyalty, and tolerance.

I say this in truth—Kathy was always there, Neal needed her.

Kathy was Neal's rock—she was the rock their marriage was built upon. She stood by him through all the problems in life, and I never heard a complaint fall from her lips.

So often, by the unspoken love of caring for Neal, Kathy made his life easier, better, and maybe even possible for so long.

As I saw Neal going downhill, I watch Kathy disassemble Neal's scooter and load it in their van: I saw her bring him plates of food and beverages at picnics, and she helped him in the bathroom.

LOVE!

As a teacher, I always told students my definition of 'Love': putting another person's welfare and happiness before your own. That is real love.

That is what Kathy did for Neal.

I can testify as well to Neal's love for Kathy. Without a doubt, he loved her dearly because I have never forgotten the time Neal came to my house in Delafield, apparently at a time of crisis in his life, and he spoke of love for Kathy with tears in his eyes while sitting at my kitchen table.

Now, as I write this eulogy, I am reminded of O'Henry's story: 'The Gift of Magi'. The characters, Jim and Della, show their love for each other by the sacrifices they make for one another.

Jim sells his prized possession: a gold watch passed on to him from his grandfather and father, so that he can buy his wife a set of combs for her long, beautiful hair.

And Della cuts and sells her most prized possession—her hair that flows to her knees—so that she can buy Jim a gold chain for his watch.
Each sacrifice for the other out of love.

So was it with Neal and Kathy, but their sacrifices were of more grit, more difficult, and of longer and greater consequence.

Their sacrifices were ongoing throughout a lifetime. That is real love.

A word to Neal's daughters: your father had a love for travel, and he often told me of your family travels throughout the country.

I respected what your parents did taking you along when you were kids. As Hollywood movies show, family vacations can be chaotic.

Now that you are adults with children of your own, I wish you fond memories of the places you went and the things you saw and did.

I wish for smiles to light your faces when you describe to your children the vacations you had with your mom and dad.

Finally, I am forever grateful to Neal that he called me in Tennessee when our friend Ed Jackamonnis died.

I don't remember if Ed's was to be the next morning or the following, but I remember driving home without stopping.

And the morning of, I met Neal at the Guesthouse where Ed's family and friends where gathered.

Were it not for Neal, I would never had been present to mourn my friend Ed and to pay my respects to his wife Barbara.

So now, when I weigh my friendship with Neal on a scale, it is closely balanced though it tilt's in Neal's favor.

I think he was a better friend to me than I was to him, though that might be because Neal has his thumb on the scale.

But that's fine with me because he was my friend.

So now, I will say goodbye, my friend. I'll see you in Heaven if I get there.

EULOGY FOR BETTY STRIKE

Good morning and welcome!

I'm Bob Hoskins, and Betty was my sister-in-law for 63 years by virtue of her marriage to Roger and my marriage to Roger's sister Janet.

My eulogy today will be to honor Betty, but also to honor her husband Roger who I knew since we were kids in 1945. And why not honor the two of them—they were a team for all those years, working the farm together. In fact, Betty spent as much time in the barn and fields with Roger as she did working in the house.

And let me say, Roger was no gentleman farmer. He knew what it was to get cow manure on his shoes, even his hands. That happens if you're a dairy farmer.

And Betty, herself, must have gotten dirt under her fingernails working outside and in the garden.

Farming is a life of work.

I went to high school with Roger, but only for one year. Actually, I went to high school with both Roger and Betty, but not in the same year and not at the same school.

In 1950. I was a freshman and Roger was a sophomore at Whitewater. Of course, we rode the school bus together every day that school year.

Well, not every day!

You see Roger got kicked off the school bus for a week because of his misbehavior. I'll bet he didn't tell his boys that.

You see, Roger got involved in a water fight on the bus with me, among others. He was caught with a squirt gun shooting at me. The bus driver apparently thought I was unarmed and only saw Roger's weapon.

But of course, others and I were just guilty—but we weren't caught. So Roger paid the penalty, which he deserved because he got me wet.

That same year in Mat 1950, Maple Grove School—which sat on land taken from the Strike farm—burned to the ground. Only the chimney stood after the fire.

Because the school was gone, all the grade school children from Maple Grove were assigned to the Palmyra District. High School students had a choice. Roger stayed at Whitewater for his junior year.

I started my sophomore year at Palmyra were Betty was a junior. Her family had a small farm near Eagle and raised vegetables which sold at the Farmers Market in West Allis.

It wasn't until the following year that Roger switched to Palmyra where he and Betty met as seniors. I wasn't there to introduce them to each other because I went to school in Madison my junior year.

By the time I returned for my senior year, Roger and Betty had graduated. I can't tell you if they dated as seniors. Nor can I say when their love became serious. I wasn't there.

So let's flash forward to 1965—Roger and Betty got married.

What can I tell you about their wedding? Nothing! I was not in the wedding party—I wasn't even in the wedding. I was spending summer at

Quantico, VA, at the Marine Corps Platoon Leaders School.

I do not even know if Roger and Betty had a honeymoon. But I do know their marriage bought big changes to the farm—running water and indoor plumbing. And the upstairs was remodeled into a separate living unit for the newlyweds.

With Betty's arrival, life in the farm became easier for everyone.
Soon, Betty was involved with more changes – like diapers! She and Roger had five boys, but Betty probably thought she counted six at the dinner table because my son Bobby spent summers and school vacations at their farm, which I thought was great because Janet and I didn't have to feed him.

One thing about Betty's boys: In those years she kept me confused. I didn't know which of her boys was which—they all had nicknames!

I didn't know if Glen, or Roger, or David was Tuff, or Herk, or Digger; only Danny was Danny!

But to be serious, I think people like Roger and Betty are the backbone of our country.
They work the farms; they grow the food that feeds the rest of us; and it is not an easy life.

They raised five boys, and as dairy farmers, they were tied to the farm for most of their life. How many vacations do you think they took over the years? How many days did they enjoy when they didn't have to lift a finger?

I can attest to their sons: your mom and dad were good people, hardworking, and neighborly. Whatever mistakes they made during their lives, whatever faults they had, Christ tells us to forgive.

So, if anyone among us carries ill-will or harbors resentment in his or her heart; you are commanded to forgive one another. As a corollary, the Ten Commandments do not suggest—they command us to honor our fathers and mothers.

So Glen, Danny, Roger, David: today we join with you to honor your mother, to pay our respects, and to recall personal memories in our lives that we shared with her.

The Betty that I knew was a person of strong views and outspoken. She was not afraid to speak her mind. In conversation, she had a voice of authority. When she called one of her boys, they heard —and they got the message. Now her life is over.

May she rest in peace with the Lord, and may she rest with those she knew and loved in her life.

Thank you all for coming.

BOB HOSKINS' REVIEW OF THE YEAR 2003 AND MERRY CHRISTMAS TO ALL!

I have been so busy these past few months, I apologize for letting Christmas slip past without a card or call to distant family members and friends.

I closed my mother's estate December 22 after she had died in March 2003. I need to rush events for a reason, so I actually went to the Department of Revenue in Madison twice in November and December and to the probate office in Waukesha to Hasten the process. In addition, I was busy with the usual Christmas activities.

After my mother's funeral March 25, which was preceded by the funeral of her brother (Uncle Gordy) the previous week March 28, I filed my taxes and took off for Nashville on April 2 with Mary Ann. My son Jim came with us, and while I attended songwriting seminars, Jim and Mary Ann went sightseeing. As usual, we listened to Bill Ferrari play piano at the Vanderbilt Hotel each night before heading to Tootsies Orchid Lounge to hear authentic country music.

On Saturday, we left Nashville and spent the night in Memphis listening to the "blues," Jim's favorite music. We left Memphis on Sunday, driving to Branson, MO, where we stayed three days attending shows, including my favorite showman, Jim Stafford (famous for writing the song: "I don't like spiders and snakes…").

Jumping ahead, after we returned home, I started making preparations for my late summer excursion. But first I had to work at the Wisconsin

State Fair, July 31 to August 10. Two days after the Fair ended, Mary Ann and I were gone in a rental car. Avis made a mistake on my reservation, so they let me have a 2003 Lincoln town car for a deal. Two weeks for $230, including the tax.

We traveled to Baltimore (a great city), stayed a night at the Renaissance Hotel on the Inner Harbor downtown, visited churches, and took a water taxi to Fort McHenry (where the rockets' red glare, showed our flag was still there). We also drove to nearby Annapolis, toured the U.S. Naval Academy, and went on a harbor cruise.

Leaving Baltimore, we drove to Philadelphia by way of Washington, Delaware, where we toured the Alfred I. du Pont Mansion. In Philadelphia, we visited most of the famous sites involved in our nation's founding. We spent our last night in King of Prussia, PA (outside of Philadelphia) before heading for the Pocono Mts. However, at breakfast, we learned that Valley Forge was about a mile from our motel. So, we took a self-guided tour before leaving that day. Of course, we left with lots of pictures for my album.

That night, we ate dinner in Jim Thorpe, PA (the town is named to honor the great athlete). This is an enchanting town to visit, a must-see if you are ever in the Poconos. The following day we visited Bushkill Falls, actually eight falls. We hiked two miles over very rough terrain, up and down a 300-foot gorge. The largest falls fell 100 feet. Because we had to rest frequently after steep climbs, the hike took a couple hours.

Bushkill Falls is aptly named, but we survived.

After the Pocono Mountains, we ended our trip at Niagara Falls, Canada, and while we were there, on the second night, the lights on the Falls were turned on after being dark for nearly a week because of the Northeast blackout. Incidentally, we were staying on the 12th floor at the Renaissance Hotel when the electricity began shutting off in New York State, Cleveland, New Jersey, and elsewhere. But the outage never reached Baltimore, so we were able to use the elevators.

On our return to the U.S. from Canada, Mary Ann was upset because we were not required to show any documents as we crossed the international border. She had her passport ready, and before we had left home, she had nagged me to find birth certificate. I did find it, but I told her I would not need it. I was right. The custom official only asked about five questions, including were we bringing any liquor into the country.

On a more serious note, a day after we crossed the border, my son Jerry and his two teenage sons coincidentally were crossing into Canada. They were detained over an hour, and the boys and Jerry were separated for interrogation because the government is very leery of a person taking children out of the U.S. in case of parent-kidnapping. If the boys had their birth certificates with them, the crossing would have been easier. My son Jerry was not at all upset because he understood the government's concern, but his boys were angry at being detained. It worked out okay; they got to see the Falls.

After returning from two weeks of travel, I was happy to be home (be it ever so humble). We had traveled through ten states and Ontario, Canada. We had stayed one night in New Jersey as one of the states I've been in.

No sooner were we home, and the 100-year Harley-Davidson celebration was beginning. I worked at State Fair Park, one of the headquarters for the event. The Harley party ended Labor Day, and schools started the next day. I began my 12th year as a substitute teacher since my retirement.

In late September, I began a two-week assignment for a teacher whose son had contracted a staph infection and had nearly died. He was one of ten members of the Franklin High School football team hit by the infection. The outbreak made the front page of USA Today as a major news story.

In October, I spent a weekend at Wisconsin Dells as a guest of a time-share resort, and the first week of November, I spent my owner's week at the Rushes Resort in Door County (near Bailey's Harbor). I had breakfast most every morning at the White Gull Inn in Fish Creek. What a way to live!

Mary Ann and I returned to the Rushes for the annual owners' party and meeting the second weekend in December. We were joined by her brother and sister-in-law who own two weeks at the Rushes. If anyone wants to join me there next year, let me know. My week will be October 30-November 6.

So this is what I have been doing in the past year of my life, 2003. I have said more than I intended when I started this missive, but then I live an exciting life, and I share it with you on paper to make you envious.

I hope you had a Blessed Christmas, and I wish you happiness in 2004.

BOB HOSKINS

BOB HOSKINS' REVIEW OF THE YEAR 2004 AND MERRY CHRISTMAS TO ALL!

In April of this year, Mary Ann and I made our annual trio to Nashville, but this year we made a side trio to Lynchburg, Tennessee (pop. 361). This metropolis is the home of JACK DANIELS DISTILLERY.

First, we had lunch/dinner at Mary Bobo's Boarding House. We were lucky; reservations are required, but they had a cancellation. Of the 10-12 people at the table, we came from five states. After dinner, we toured Jack Daniels, which was very interesting. Though they cannot serve or sell whiskey per local law, they did serve lemonade and coffee. I had at least ten glasses of a very thirst-quenching lemonade. However, the distillery is allowed to sell a commemorative bottle by passage of a state law.

I bought a bottle!

In June, as soon as the schools were out, Mary Ann and I headed west. I rented a Cadillac for two weeks. The ride was so smooth, I often caught myself going 90 mph. (The speed limit is 75 mph in some states.) Finally, I decided to put the car up to 100 when I caught my speed at 94. I put the peddle down further, but I could not get past 99 mph. The rental agency must have some device to limit the speed. So, I let up.

We want west because I want to see every state in the contiguous forty-eight. I had never been to Ohio, Oregon, or Washington. After them, the New England states are the only ones left to see.

On the way, we stopped at Mt. Rushmore, the Devil's Tower Monument, the Buffalo Bill Cody Museums in Cody, WY, and Yellowstone an Zion Parks. We stayed in Jackson Hole for an extra day and took a floating raft trip on the Snake River (not on white water!). From there, we hit my first destination: Idaho. We stayed in Boise and took a trolley tour. Nice city!

Leaving Boise, we traveled the Columbia River Gorge. Magnificent natural beauty! We stopped at Troutdale, OR, about 15 miles east Portland. How fortunate! There is a great restaurant (also resort) where I had one of the best meals of my life: plank steak. The name of the place is McMenamin's Edgefield. The place is a historic treasure.

In the morning, we backtracked ten miles to see a series of waterfalls. We saw four, including Multnomah Falls. It cascades 620 feet down Larch Mountain. That afternoon, we visited the Japanese Gardens and the Rose Gardens in Portland. Definitely visit these gardens if you are in Portland. They adjoin each other. We finished the day by driving to Bellevue, WA, where my son Jerry had found a reservation at the Hyatt Hotel for less than $90 a night, saving us over $300 for the two nights.

In Seattle, we visited the Pike Place Market, took the Duck tour, ate lunch at the top of the Space Needle, and took a ferry boat to San Juan Islands. What a bargain! The ferry trip tales about an hour each way at a cost of $5 round trip. Of course, if we took the car, add another $40. Still not bad.

On our way back to Wisconsin, we made a short side trip to Grand Coulee Dam. At the visitor center, I was told that airlines like those that flew into the Trade Centers would hardly make a dent. The dam is built 20,000,000 tons of concrete (two to three times that of Hoover Dam). It is nearly a mile wide, and it creates a lake that extends 151 miles.

We stayed the night in Coeur D'Alene, ID. We had breakfast at the Coeur D'Alene Resort. It costs as much as $549 for a night. We didn't stay there. After we left Coeur D'Alene, we drove to Big Timber, Montana. We ate dinner at the old west hotel. Mary Ann had been to the town 20 years earlier, but she hardly recognized the place. I guess the town had gotten older. Our last night on the road we spent in Sioux Falls, S. Dakota.

Next year: New England here we come, but only after Quebec and Montreal, Canada before aiming for Maine.

In August, I worked at the State Fair again on the trams. I have now attended the Fair 56 straight years from 1948 to 2004.

In October, my sisters Kathy and Nancy (with Tom), and our Aunt Lona rented a van for a trip to Branson, MO. We stayed overnight at Our Lady of the Snow, a Catholic shrine in Illinois, across the river from St Louis. They have a nice hotel. The following day, we traveled the rest of the way to Branson where we met our sister Laura and Ray.

Among the shows, the best were Jim Stafford by consensus, Yakov Smirnoff (a close second), and Shoji Tabuchi (the Japanese violinist). Some of us saw other shows, but they did not rank with these three.

By the way, we all stayed at the same motel in Branson. It was a wonderful Family event for all of us with conversation all the way and some good meals at Cracker Barrel Restaurant. Incidentally, we were joined in Branson by Mary Ann's sister Kathy and her husband Dick who coincidentally have two daughters: Debbie and Cherie, the same as my sister Kathy and her ex-husband Dick.

In late October-November, I spent my week at the Rushes in Door County. We were joined for one day by Mary Ann's brother Bob and his wife Helen who live in Green Bay. None of my family or relatives joined us, though they have standing invitations.

December 18 finds my son Jerry graduating from Cardinal Stritch University after years of night and weekend classes. Good going, Jerry!

On January 2, Mary Ann and I will be having our Christmas party starting anytime after 1:00 pm, and if you are still hanging around after 8:30 pm, we will be calling the police to get you to go home. On the menu will be chili again. If you were at the party last year, you may remember that the big burner on my electric, glass top stove cracked and burned a hole in the bottom of the chili kettle. Recently, I replaced the glass top on my stove. Cost $265. You can see why I delayed buying a new one.

So I have given you your marching orders. We rendezvous Sunday, January 2nd at Camp Scepter Dr., 7871 South. To reach command center, call (414) 529-7049.

BOB HOSKINS' REVIEW OF THE YEAR 2005 AND MERRY CHRISTMAS TO ALL

It was a sad year. I was not even going to write a yearned message.

In July, we traveled to Marion, Iowa for the funeral of our cousin, Bob Hoskins. On August 25, our sister Nancy Niese finally succumbed to cancer, and tragically, Mary Ann's grandson died September 3 in Afghanistan where he was serving in the U.S. Marine Corps. Ryan Nass had just turned age 21 on August 26th.

Life for the rest of us went on.

In April, Mary Ann, her daughter Lisa, her friend Peter, and I went to Nashville. I went there on songwriting business, the others for pleasure. Of course, we ended up at Tootsie's Orchid Lounge much of the time to hear true country music and to join the revelry. Mary Ann and I stayed at the Maxwell House (well known for the coffee it serves).

For the information of all you tea-drinkers, Teddy Roosevelt was at the Maxwell House, and when he got up from the table, he finished his coffee saying: "Good to the last drop!" thereby coining one of the great advertising slogans.

After, Nashville, daily routine and sadness dominated our life until September 23 when Mary Ann and I left on an extended trip to Canada and New England. We traveled by the way of Niagara Falls where we spent a day. On Sunday, we drove to Montreal, going through metro- Toronto. (What

god-awful traffic for a Sunday!)
I am not an admirer of French culture, including French cuisine. But French Catholics sure know how to build magnificent churches. In Montreal, we visited St. Joseph's Oratory which had not been on my list to see. It was only because a hotel clerk told me, "You must see it." So we went, which was fortuitous, because the Oratory truly is magnificent to see.

The Oratory sits on a high hill overlooking a large area of Montreal. And it is actually two churches on the site, with the second church built atop the lower church. Inside the Oratory is a room filled with canes and crutches left behind by disabled worshipers, who apparently, by faith and prayer, were able to leave behind their appliances.

We left Montreal in the afternoon to drive to Quebec by nightfall. The following day, we drove to St. Anne de Beaupre to see that church, somewhat like driving out from Milwaukee to Holy Hill. A train also takes pilgrims and tourists from Quebec virtually to the church visitor center. At St. Anne, Mary Ann and I attended Mass. Afterward, we followed the Way of the Cross along a hillside, simulating the journey of Christ as he made His way to Cavalry. Later that day, before leaving, Mary Ann and I both climbed the stairs to an outdoor shrine on hands and knees—a tradition at St. Anne de Beaupre.

On the way back to Quebec, we detoured across a long bridge over the Saint Lawrence River to the Isle of Orleans. I loved the island. It reminded me of Door County in Wisconsin. We stopped at an ice cream shoppe where I had raisin rum, most delicious! Around the corner of the building was a chocolate shoppe. We had indeed found Paradise! And twenty miles in the distance, the Quebec skyline loomed across a very wide St. Lawrence River.

The next day, we walked along the fortress wall of the Old City where General James Wolfe led his British troops against the French in the 1950's. His men reached the Plains of Abraham thereby capturing Quebec, but Wolfe was fatally wounded in the battle.

For lunch, we ate at a sidewalk cafe. In between, we explored Quebec's many narrow side streets, and Mary Ann bought a painting of a Quebec street scene at one of the many galleries that line the streets. As for me, I got into an argument at the local post office because they charged me sales tax on the postage stamps I had bought. Something we don't do in the USA.

So now it was goodbye Canada. Hello Maine and the USA!

Maine was nothing but forest for a hundred miles, but I don't recall seeing a single deer-crossing sign. Instead, moose-crossing signs were everywhere, though we did not see any moose. We were going to stay at Old Orchard Beach on the Atlantic Ocean, but the place was virtually deserted because the summer season was over, and it was now September 29, So instead, we drove to New Hampshire for the night.

The following day, we drove the length of the State through the White Mountains, ending the day in Montpelier, Vermont, the capitol of that state. Absolutely no motel rooms were available in the town; it was a Friday night, and we ended up in a very expensive, but rundown motel in a nearby town.

Saturday was a beautiful autumn day. We visited a maple sugar farm, then on to Ben and Jerry's ice cream plant, the biggest tourist attraction in Vermont. After eating free samples of their offerings, we headed to a big cider mill and store about three miles down the road. Buy a cup for 90¢ and you could drink cider all day.

We left Montpelier that afternoon and drove to Massachusetts, the Concord/Lexington area, outside Boston. To prove how smart I am, I decided to drive into Boston on Sunday morning, stay overnight in a motel near the downtown, then drive back to Concord on Monday morning. I zoomed into Boston at 60-70 miles per hour with hardly any traffic.

On Monday morning, having spent Sunday in Boston where we ate dinner at Pier 4 on the water, we drove out of Boston (instead of driving in) and I congratulate myself as we passed mile, after a mile, after mile, after a mile of traffic at a virtual standstill heading into downtown. That mess could have included me. Instead, I had open roads since few people commute out of Boston on weekdays heading to Concord.

Concord is where the American Revolutionary War began. What a great New England town, lots of charm. It was the early literary capital of our nation: Ralph Waldo Emerson, Nathaniel Hawthorne, Louisa May Alcott, and Henry David Thoreau all lived there. Thoreau wrote the book every student use to read: Walden. He spent a year living at Walden Pond in a cabin he built. Walden Pond is a mile or so from the center of Concord and is actually a small lake. People were still swimming in it on October 1. That tells you the weather we were having. I took a picture of Mary Ann standing in its waters and then dipped my hands into the holy waters as well. After a brief stop at the Lexington Green, we headed to Plymouth Rock, south of Boston.

Plymouth Rock is more like Plymouth Stone. It is not worth the trip unless you want to see a replica of the Mayflower. It was a short drive to Providence, Rhode Island where we stayed that night.

In the morning, we were to head to Connecticut. We got as far as Narragansett, RI where we had lunch at the old Coast Guard station on the bay. As I paid my bill, I saw the high-water mark of Hurricane Bob by the entrance. It was several feet up the wall near the ceiling. Naturally, I could not pass up a picture with my namasake on the wall. The mark had to be at least 20 feet above sea level and eight feet above the outside street level.

At Mary Ann's insistence, we decided to cross Narragansett Bay to Newport, RI, the summer home of the Vanderbilts. Various family members had to built several mansions which you can tour. Late that afternoon, we were sitting at an open bar on one of the wharves. As we talked to a local couple, we asked the name of the restaurant they would recommend. It turned out that the fellow owned a restaurant named Cheeky Monkey on a nearby wharf. He took out his business card and wrote us a gift certificate for $40 at his restaurant. Nice, Huh?

I have one of his business cards and will be contacting him this week. Hank Kates is his name. Tell him I sent you if you go to Newport. Needless to say, Mary Ann loved Newport and wants to go back. I would go with her. It is a great place to visit: nice restaurants, near the water, and shops on a small streets.

From Newport, we headed to Mystic, Connecticut, the home of Mystic Pizza and the setting for the movie of the same name which starred Julia Roberts. Of course, we had pizza while we were there. About 10 miles north is the biggest gambling casino in North America operated by an Indian tribe. It is huge, and just about 20 miles away is a casino of the Mohicans. (Yes, they are still around.) What a beautiful complex of buildings, but not as big.

In honor of Uncle Gordy, we visited the Coast Guard Academy. We were able to drive around the grounds and tour the library, but they do not have tours like the Naval Academy in Annapolis, Maryland. We later toured the USS Nautilus submarine and the Museum in Groton, CT.

Coventry, CT is the home of Nathan Hale whose only regret was that he had but one life to give for his country. Since I do most of my substitute teaching at Nathan Hale High School in West Allis, I naturally had to make a pilgrimage to Hale's birthplace.

In New Haven, CT, we toured Yale University which impressed me beyond any measure. What a school! its law school is number one in the nation and what a list of graduates: Pres. George Bush, Pres. Bill Clinton, Pres. George W. Bush, and maybe Pres. Hillary Clinton, plus Pres. Gerald Ford and our own Sen. Bill Proxmire.

And the Yale School of Drama: what an illustrious bill of actors have come from there. On that list is David Hyde-Pierce who plays Niles Crane on "Frasier". His character could have graduated from Yale just as well.

Then there is Nathan Hale, also a graduate of Yale just before the Revolutionary War. When George Washington needed to spy on the British in New York, Hale volunteered. He was captured, hanged, and buried in an unknown grave somewhere in that city.

Nobody knows what Hale looked like since he never had his portrait painted; hence when Yale commissioned a statue for its campus, they assembled the freshmen class and selected one student to be the model. An exact copy of the statue stands at the CIA Headquarters in Langley, VA. New Haven was our last stop on our vacation. Form there we headed home. We went north to bypass New York City, crossed the Hudson River, and drove across New Jersey. As we approached the Delaware Gap where New Jersey and Pennsylvania are separated by the Delaware River, it began to rain. The clouds in the low mountains were ominous as darkness was descending, so after 20 miles I stopped for the night at the exact motel where Mary Ann and I had stayed two years earlier. Pulling off the road at that exit had been just by chance.

The next day we drove the distance across Pennsylvania and the rest of the way home. We drove the first 500 miles to Cleveland in the rain. We had ended our trip in the Northeast just in time because you may recall the rains continued for a week, and many places we had been had severe flooding. Home sweet, Home!

Well, now I can say I have been to every state in the Union, except the 49th and 50th states. New England was the only area that had remained on my agenda, and I have now driven to every one. No cheating going by airplane, I have actually slept and eaten in all forty-eight.

I did not use my time-share in Door County this year. I rented my week for $500 which helped pay for my trip. Next year, if anyone wants to join me at the Rushes on Kangaroo Lake, let me know early enough.

Life is not without cost. I have worked every day that a job was available at the three schools where I substitute-teach. But I am happy. I hope you are. Merry Christmas and a prosperous New Year to all.

P.S. I have a postscript.

I almost forgot an important event of this year. My granddaughter Octavia and Mike Haines got married. Her name is now Haines. On the day of the wedding, a tornado watch was in effect for Jefferson County. As we were coming through Jefferson, the sirens went off.

The wedding was planned for outdoors at the farm of Michael's aunt in Fort Atkinson, the next town to the west. What was the situation at her farm? Always the believer, I looked to Heaven and prayed to Octavia's (great) Grandmother Izzy, her (great) Gramps Bert, and her (great) Uncle Gordy—all of whom loved Tavia dearly. Within minutes, the skies cleared and the sun came over.

The power of prayer!

For the next several hours, even the rain held off. We later learned that a tornado took part of the roof off Jefferson High School and had passed within half a mile of where we were stopped off the highway.

Octavia and Mike were married on June 4, 2005.

Addendum

I WAS REQUESTED BY MY DAUGHTER ELIZABETH TO LIST MY
LIFE ACCOMPLISHMENTS. INSTEAD, I HAVE DECIDED TO LIST
THE THINGS I DID IN MY LIFE OF WHICH I AM PROUD TO HAVE
DONE. HERE IS THE LIST AS I HAVE DETERMINED IT.

I

As a student in the 8th grade, at the age of 13, I was Keeper of the Flame.
Each morning , the winter 1948-49, I walked from our farm to our one-room
rural school in Jefferson County where I made the fire. At 7:00 AM,
I arrived an hour before the teacher and the other students so that we did not
freeze with only a wood stove to warm the building.

I am proud that I was trusted and responsible --- at age 13

AND... I had a key to the school!

I am proud too that I was a member of 4-H (Head, Heart, Hands, and Health).
My brother and I showed our Brown Swiss calves at the Jefferson Co. Fair,
both of us receiving 2nd place ribbons. Not bad, except that only three
Brown Swiss calves were entered in our class at the Fair.

I am proud that I was ---

1. Attended Queen of Apostles Seminary – even if only for a year.
2. Graduated from the U.S. Marine Corps Platoon Leaders School,
   Quantico, Va.
3. Gave up my job at Carroll College for my brother so he could go to
   Carroll.

4. Graduated from Carroll College (not the University) and am a proud Pioneer – Class of 1957.

5. Received the Stigma Tau Delta Award for best student in the English Department at Carroll College. (now Carroll University) 1957.

6. Scored 610 on the Graduate Record Exam in Education, the highest score ever recorded at Carroll – and perhaps in the nation since 610 exceeds the 597 score for the 97th percentile, the highest score stated for the test.

7. Awarded a Fellowship in American History by the University of Iowa Graduate School in 1957.

8. Selected in the first class of honorees inducted into the Palmyra-Eagle High School Wall of Fae.

9. Appointed Executive Secretary of the State Bingo Control Board from a field of more than 90 applicants after bingo gambling was legalized in Wisconsin in 1974.

10. Taught English at Oconomowoc High School from 1961 to 1974; later taught ED (Emotionally Disabled) students 1980 to 1988; and taught English and U.S. History at Lady Pitts – a school for teen-mothers in Milwaukee – 1988-92.

    As a teacher at Oconomowoc High School, I am proud that I took my students on fields trips to see movies of worth that they might not ordinarily go to see. A list of movies includes: 'Julius Caesar', 'Sounder', 'Jesus Christ Superstar', 'The effect of Gamma Rays on Man-in-the-moon Marigolds', and 'West Side story'.

    Moreover, I am just as proud of the books we read in my classes. A list includes: One Day in the Life of Ivan Denisovich, Black Boy, Of Mice and Men, Hot Rod, Visit to a Small Planet, Julius Caesar, West Side story, and Great Expectations.

11. Conducted eight political campaigns for election – 5 as a Democrat and 3 on the Republican ticket after changing political parties – lost every race.

12. Endorsed three times by the Milwaukee Journal for election to the Wisconsin Legislature.

13. Turned down political contributions in 1972 which were offered in return for changing my position on abortion from pro-life to pro-choice.

14. Elected chairman of the Waukesha County Democratic Party. 1966

15. Selected as an Alternate Delegate from the State of Wisconsin to the 1968 Democratic National Convention held in Chicago, Il.

16. Selected for Who's Who in American Politics.

17. Graduated from the University of Wisconsin-Milwaukee with a Masters Degree in Political Science. 1968

18. Employed as a caseworker by the Waukesha County Welfare Department 1958-60. Received letter of commendation.

19. Awarded a stipend from the State of Wisconsin to attend the UW-M School of Social Work.

20. Was a personal friend of State Representative Ed Jackamonis, Speaker of the Wisconsin State Assembly, and Jim Buckley who served Gov. Pat Luccy, was a candidate for Congress, and later became a longtime lobbyist at the Capitol.

21. Attended a White House Conference in Milwaukee with President Gerald Ford; also throughout career, shook hands with Adali Stevenson, Hubert Humphrey, John F. Kennedy, Bobby Kennedy, Eugene McCarthy, and Ted Kennedy --- all of them candidates for President of the United States.

22. Was on a first-name basis with Secretary of Defense Les Aspin, Governors Patrick Lucey and Martin Schreiber, and Governor Tommy Thompson who once told me: "Bob, you should have been in the Legislature!" to which I replied: "Yes, I should have been – and I tried."

23. Invited by Jay Sykes, a writer and editor at the Milwaukee Sentinel, to attend a news conference with Ellen McCormack of Massachusetts when she was running for U.S. President. (She autographed an anti-abortion letter that I wrote.)

    Jay honored me a second time: he asked me to nominate his 13 year old son, Charlie, to be a page at the 1968 Democratic National Convention --- we were both delegates. I nominated Charlie, who was elected, and later had a distinguished career as an author of several books and as a talk-show host.

    I am proud that Jay trusted and respected me in selecting me from the Wisconsin delegation to nominate his son.

24. Introduced John Lindsay of New York at a dinner in Waukesha when

Lindsay was running for U.S. President.

25. Sought election to Chief Clerk of the Wisconsin State of Assembly losing by one vote.

26. Wrote the law that legalized raffles for charitable purposes in Wisconsin, working with State Representative Steve Gunderson who was later elected to Congress representing the La Crosse area and western Wisconsin.

27. Worked for State Representative Lew Mittness and Fred Kessler, Chairman of the Natural Resources and State Affairs Committees respectively in the Legislature.

28. Appointed by Governor Tommy Thompson to serve as a public member of the Wisconsin Land Surveyors Board; the Wisconsin Senate confirmed the appointment by a vote of 27-0.

29. Served as President of the Holy Name Society for two years at St. Jerome Catholic Parish in Oconomowoc, WI.

30. Member of the Nashville Songwriters Association (NSAI) and wrote the lyrics for a music CD, Chasing Rainbows; also composed the melody for three of the songs. (The song "One Last Time" was sold to a movie.)

31. Wrote <u>Pieces of My Life</u>, a book of poetry and selected non-poetry writings: letters, speeches, eulogies, and reviews.

32. Sang the National Anthem at the Holiday Folk Fair for the Naturalized Citizen Ceremony attended by more than 100 new citizens-to-be, their families, and friends. (2018)

33. Carried the American flag as a member of the U.S. Marine color guard to lead the Reeseville (WI) Centinnial Parade. (1956)

34. Choose six granddaughters to serve as pallbearers at my mother's funeral.

35. Proudly attended St. Michaels's Catholic Grade School in Milwaukee for 3rd and 4th grades and Maple Grove, a one-room rural school in Jefferson Co., where I completed grades 5th-8th with the same teacher, Ida Boneck.

36. Survived Beta Pi Epsilon HELL WEEK – the Betas were the oldest and proudest Greek fraternity at Carroll College, founded May 6, 1906, but were banned from campus in the 2000's.

37. Lettered in football at Carroll College – and at Palmyra High School

where the team played six-man football. Also played on the Carroll freshman basketball team and was awarded a numeral sweater.

38. Selected as the escort for the Carroll Homecoming Queen at the halftime program of the football game in our senior year. Both the Queen and I were on crutches – she with a broken foot and I with a broken leg suffered in a football game earlier that season.

39. Performed as a stuntman in the movie 'Gaily, Gaily' directed by Norman Jewison – who also directed 'Fiddler on the Roof', 'The Russians are Coming', and 'Jesus Christ, Superstar'.

40. Applied and presented myself at the Chicago Sun Times as a replacement for syndicate advice-columnist, Ann Landers.

41. Personal driver for actor Paul Newman when he campaigned for U.S. Senator Eugene McCarthy in the 1968 Wisconsin Presidential Primary Election. Newman complimented me as the best driver he had in the campaign.

42. Present in Senator Eugene McCarthy's suite at the Hilton Hotel in Chicago in 1968, the night McCarthy was nominated for President of the United States.

43. Umpired baseball for the Waukesha Co. Recreational Department more than 25 years. Additionally, umpired WIAA high school baseball and girls' softball in the 1980's, and umped a season for the Land O'Lakes at the request of League Commission Johnny Nelson.

44. Supervised the Oconomowoc High School intramural basketball and football programs and was a faculty advisor for the school newspaper.

45. Judged high school debate and forensics at tournaments for more than a decade while a teacher at Oconomowoc, and continued to be a judge after my appointment as state Bingo Secretary.

46. Served as the treasurer of Unlimited Jazz Limited – a Southeastern Wisconsin music organization of jazz aficionados dedicated to the preservation of jazz as a music form.

47. Selected as a finalist for the position of Milwaukee County Economic Development Liaison 'out of nearly 100 candidates'. (Someone better got the position.)

48. Invited by songwriter Alex Harvey and his wife to sit with them at the Reserved Table during an NSAI Showcase at the Vanderbilt Hotel in Nashville (July 1993). Harvey was the M.C. for the Showcase, and

performed two songs he had written – 'Delta Dawn'.

Both songs were huge hits — Kenny Rogers recorded 'Ruben Jam'. and Helen Reddy recorded 'Delta Dawn'.

49. Had my picture taken with Faye Dunaway, who starred in the movie 'Bonnie and Clyde' – she played Bonnie – and I still have the picture which she autographed.

50. Worked at the Wisconsin State Fair: summers, fair week, and weekends for more than 25 years. Mostly, I worked Security for the grandstand and stage, race track, coliseum, and RV office. In the RV office, I worked full time during the months of the year the office was open; and it was there I exchanged jokes with the academy award-actor Earnest Borgnine who starred in such movies as 'Marty', 'From Here to Eternity', 'Marvin Gardens', and the TV series 'McHale's Navy'.

51. Following my retirement as a teacher at age 56, I continued to teach as a substitute teacher in five Milwaukee County school districts until age 84, finally deciding to hang it up when the covid-19 pandemic began in China in November, 2019. Later, I thought about going back to substituting, but I decided that I didn't want to be another Tom Brady!

TO CONCLUDE, I AM LISTING THE THINGS THAT I DID (WHICH WERE THE SOURCES OR ORIGIN OF MY MOTIVATION AND CONSCIENCE) THAT LED ME TO DO THE THINGS OF WHICH I AM PROUD.

52. As a boy at the age of ten, continuing until I left for college at seventeen, I worked on the family farm: hauling hay, shocking oats, husking corn (by hand), cutting thistles and pulling weeds. I climbed hay lofts and siloes to feed farm animals; I cleaned cow barns, calf pens, chicken coops, pig pens, and horse stalls; and I picked apples, cherries, pears, and vegetables from the orchard and garden. Along the way, I learned to drive a team of horses and a tractor.

Also, as a teenager, worked on the local threshing crew going to neighboring farms, and I helped on the two family milk routes, hauling milk from farms in the Jefferson County area, to Hoards Creamy in Fort Atkinson and to Hawthorne Melody in Whitewater, WI.

53. Worked on a truck farm at age 16, planting asparagus roots, weeding onion fields, and working on a hay baler.

54. Worked at Whitewater Foundry the summer after high school graduation making the sand mixture for the core makers and pulling the core racks from the ovens.

55. Worked three summers during college at Larson Canning Co. in Fort Atkinson: loading railroad cars, cooking the brine for the beets and sweet corn, and finally working in the lab recording data from the production lines.

56. In my sophomore year at Carroll, started working at the United Restaurant and the Five Point Bar which were owned by Ab Kuenzli (Abner) who became my dearest friend in life. I was a waiter, short order cook, and bartender (part-time and full time for more than 15 years - even after graduating from college.

57. While I worked at the United Restaurant, I also set pins at a bowling alley two nights a week in my junior year; I hauled mail from Soo Line depot to the Waukesha Post Office three mornings a week, rising at 3:30 AM to meet the 4:00 AM and 6:00 AM trains.

58. Additionally, I worked at Roxo Soda Water the summer before my senior year, and during Christmas vacation the same year.

59. The summer I graduated, I worked full time for Cleminshaw Appraisal Co. of Cleveland, OH, reappraising the Clay of Waukesha, the Village of Elm Grove, and the City of Wisconsin Rapids before leaving for graduate school at Iowa in late September 1957.
    The Spring of 1958, after I had returned to Waukesha, I worked for the Waukesha City Assessors Office part-time doing unfinished appraisal work.

THE FINAL THINGS IN MY LIFE OF WHICH I AM PROUD

60. As I near the end of my list, it is time to state I am proud of the family with whom I grew up, first in a house on Walnut Street in Milwaukee, and then on a farm in Jefferson County, following the death of my father, Gerald Hoskins, a factory worker at Cutler-Hammer during his short-lived life.
    I will forever remember him trimming our Christmas tree; coming

home from work with his black lunch bucket; and drinking beer at the corner tavern: He smoked Chesterfield cigarettes, drank eggnog the last weeks of his life, and had converted to Roman Catholicism to marry our mother. He attended Mass faithfully every Sunday with our mother; and lastly had many, many friends who loved him and stayed loyal to his memory for years after his death.

The rest of the family included myself, Larry, Nancy, and Kathy; then Laura and 'Jerry' (Gilbert) in the order of our births. All of us were high achievers in school and out of school.

Nevertheless, we recognize that much of what we achieved as individuals, we owe to our strong Catholic mother, who carried the many crosses of life without a murmur. We also owed much to our stepfather, Gilbert Wendt, a farmer and milk hauler, who provided us with the necessities of life, and who I came to love and called 'Dad'.

61. Finally I am proud of my children: Robert, Elizabeth, Pamela, Rebecca, Gerald and James (listed in the order of their birth); and I include my granddaughter, Octavia, whom my wife and I also raised, and who calls us Mom and Dad since all the other kids did.

All our children graduated from high school in four years, passed their drivers license test the first time; and are employed. They read books, think independently, an vote. And all of them married someone they loved though life hasn't worked out as they hoped in all cases.

And I am especially proud of my 35 year of marriage to my ex-wife, Janet Hoskins (nee Strike), my high school sweetheart and the mother of my children, whom I first met when I was nine years old. She was walking on an asphalt road, bringing a pan of beans from her family's garden, and I was sent by mother to meet her halfway. She was the neighbor girl from the farm next door, located in the Towns of Sullivan and Palmyra, in Jefferson County, WI.

During our marriage, she was with me in the hard times.

62. I end this list from my life with the affirmation of my love for Mary Ann Aimers – I am proud that she has allowed me to share her life for the past 31 years. My love for her has endured, and she has kept me on the right path.

But I am not blind to her faults. As an example, Mary Ann is an excellent speller (as she often reminds me). Knowing this, I rely on her as my personal spell-checker, but she thinks I don't appreciate or acknowledge her contribution.

Well, I am an excellent speller myself and reply that I am only confirming my own spelling is correct--- which is usually the case.

So, Mary Ann, to keep the peace, here is a toast to "tintinnabulation', aficionados', 'timbre', and 'mnemonic'; but not to 'Cathlic', 'Luthern', or 'sophmore'!

My thanks to Mary Ann for her love, support, spelling skills, and her sense of humor --- I hope!

And to all other readers who have worked in a coal mine, or a cotton mill, or on a farm making hay or threshing grain --- check with your doctor. You may have a disease of the lungs, associated with coughing and environmental dust, commonly known as "pneumonoultramicroscopicsilicovolcaneconiosis".

SPELL THAT MARY ANN!

CONCLUSION: A PRAYER OF THANKSGIVING

I give thanks to God that the places I worked, people with whom I worked, and the skills and knowledge I acquired prepared me for a life that many think is a life of accomplishment.

The lesson I learned in working, taught me respect for others, cooperation, the need for honesty in dealing with people, empathy, and a multitude of such other virtues. From these lessons, I acquired values, beliefs, and confidence which I used in setting goals and pursuing them.

And because I worked, and because I persisted, and because I had the support of others, I was able to achieve my goals. The goals became my accomplishments.

Now, my hope is that my children, and their descendants who follow, will continue to hold the values, beliefs, and dreams that I have tried to uphold – but hopefully, with more success than I.

May they all serve God and their fellow man with distinction in everything they do in their lives.

AMEN!